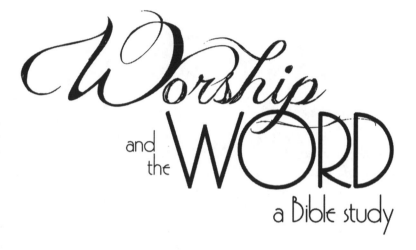

Worship and the WORD
a Bible study

Pamela Haddix

D1089288

earthwhile
publishing

Blessings . . .

I've been so very blessed to serve alongside my husband, John, in music and worship ministry from the time when we first met throughout our married lives. His love encourages me, and his faith and gifts inspire me. And I've had the pleasure of being led to the throne by him on most Sunday mornings over the past 25 years. Thank you, honey, for showing me daily who our Heavenly Father is and how faithfully He loves by leading and loving me so very well. And thank you for encouraging and helping me along this journey - (especially with that first rough draft). What an amazing gift you are to me. I love you so.

My heart is also filled and inspired by the love and faith of our two daughters and their husbands - Lindsy and Jordan, and Krista and Ben. God out-did Himself (as if He really could) when He gave me you. You truly help me see more of Him – and you just make me smile. (Giving us Jude and Isaac doesn't hurt either, Linds.) Girls, thank you for your support and help with this project – especially, Lindsy, for your work on that first edit, and both of you for answering those emails asking for help with words when my brain had just gone numb. Couldn't love you more.

And I mustn't neglect a moment like this to remember my precious grandmother, Effert Lewis, who read the word of God to me often when I was young and who I know prayed for me much more. She was the first example of a truly God-seeking woman that I had in this life. (I can hear her singing hymns from her kitchen now.) I can't wait to see you and worship our God beside you again one day, Granny. Thanks for leaving me your well-worn, note-filled Bible.

Finally – only You, my Awesome God, could raise something like this out of this bowed-down, humbled-before-You, unworthy-apart-from-You, still-learning, still-growing person that I am. Only You could take someone who absolutely hated writing papers in school and give them a driving passion to communicate through the written word. (Yes, I know Your sense of humor well.) So I ask that You would work through this life's journey that You've had me on and use this resulting work in the life of another – so they can experience the absolute joy and fulfillment of worshiping You with abandon that I've come to know. You are far greater than I could ever comprehend or communicate. May I stay bowed before You.

~ Pam/Mom

Do you want to get tips or share ideas on leading others through this study? Or do you just want to join in a conversation about worship?

Check out my *Worship and the Word* facebook page or visit www.pamelahaddix.com.

I look forward to hearing from you!

CONTENTS

PRELUDE

Ascribe to the LORD, O families of the peoples,
Ascribe to the LORD glory and strength.
Ascribe to the LORD the glory of His name;
Bring an offering and come into His courts.
Worship the LORD in holy attire;
Tremble before Him, all the earth.

Psalm 96:7-9

Lesson One

PRELUDE to a Journey

"It is certainly true that hardly anything is missing from our churches these days – except the most important thing. We are missing the genuine and sacred offering of ourselves and our worship to the God and Father of our Lord Jesus Christ . . . Worship acceptable to God is the missing crown jewel in evangelical Christianity."[1]

A.W. Tozer

A.W. Tozer's words about today's Christian church are strong, and I believe they're true. If they are true, how do we find, return, and rightfully cherish the crown jewel that is "worship acceptable to God?" (as in Romans 12:2). It's my conviction that all followers of Jesus must embark on a worship journey – and a life-long one at that. It's the most important journey we'll ever take, and it's one that impacts every other venture, big or small, that we find ourselves in along the way. It's a journey that knows no bounds in its significance nor on its impact in our lives. And it's a journey that has no limits and yet has very firm limitations. It has no limits, because the object of our worship, God Himself, is limit*less*. And it has firm limitations, because not everyone can come. Oh, don't get me wrong; everyone is invited. More than that, everyone's presence is longed for by the One True God, who desires – no, is *jealous* for – our worship. And those of us who choose to accept the invitation to be a God worshiper can expect an adventure like none other. It will find us exploring His unsearchableness and pausing often to respond to His indescribableness. The only map is the Word of God, and our only guide is the Holy Spirit.

This study is the result of my growing passion to expose the veil that hides people's understanding and experience of worship, so it can be lifted, as mine has begun to be. I come to this place still a student, knowing that I won't fully grasp it all until I finally arrive at the biggest worship service imaginable. And I can't wait!

My story: A number of years ago, I attended a three-day conference that set in motion a new journey of my heart, mind, and soul to better understand what the Bible teaches about worship. I was amazed to find myself so intensely on this journey, because I thought I understood all there was to know about worship, since I had been extremely involved in it for years and enjoyed it so much. But I went into this conference carrying quite a few burdens: a difficult physical struggle, extended family health problems, and family and friends going through the rigors of divorce and custody issues. I walked in there exhausted – physically, mentally, and emotionally – from it all. However, that all changed dramatically while I was there, and I knew why.

You see, we were led in not only incredible, Spirit-led worship each day, but we worshiped for an hour or more, three-times a day, for each of those days. I really believe we worshiped for at least twelve hours in that short three-day conference! And each of those hours found me closer to the throne of God, with a clearer view of who He was in all His glory, and craving more. The result was an incredible peace that flooded my heart and mind, even as I considered all of the various problems that surrounded me and my loved ones. The change was so profound that I knew that I couldn't ignore the powerful effect of gazing intensely at my Lord and offering to Him all I could in worship.

I left there thinking, *Wow, what just happened? And what happened when people in the Bible worshiped? How can I become that kind of worshiper regularly?* I suddenly had such an incredible, inner drive to understand God's plan for me as His worshiper, that I began my study immediately. I started with finding any story I could in scripture where people worshiped. And I must admit that even after being a Christian for over twenty years at that point, and after being in vocational music ministry for close to that, I was still amazed at what I discovered. Maybe my heart and mind were just finally sensitive enough to get a deeper understanding of something I had been taught before. Or maybe it was being in a different place in life's journey that showed me my need. Regardless, it's changed my view of God, my relationship to God – my life. Am I saying that I had never worshiped or been a worshiper before? Not at all. I *am* saying that I didn't regularly get to that place of truly transforming worship nearly often enough for a variety of reasons, and therefore, I was missing out on much of God's plan for me as His child. And I don't want to go back there.

Before I begin with the definition of worship, I want to make a distinction between *praise* and *worship*. Simply, *praise* is *about* God, exalting Him for others to hear. We read in Psalm 66:8, *"Let the sound of His praise be heard." Praise* is not a difficult concept to understand, for we praise our children when they do something well. We praise each other for accomplishments or good deeds. So we, too, praise God for all that He is and has done, either to Him or to others. This comes easily, the more we grow to recognize His absolute greatness and to see its impact in and around our lives.

It is harder to define *worship*, for there are few human words to adequately capture the experience. But unlike praise, worship is always a vertical, intimate communion with the heart of God, setting our spirit free to intimately and humbly respond to His Spirit. It is to God and for His ears only. Praise and worship often go hand in hand, for when we find ourselves praising the glories of our matchless God, it often prepares and compels us to bow our hearts in worship.

While my focus in this book is on worship, you'll hear both words being used, sometimes interchangeably, depending on the source. That being said . . .

Worship Definition:
In the Old Testament we see several Hebrew words used for worship, and most of them have far more original meaning than how they are generally translated in English, so much more depth than I could convey here. Some of these are:

HALAL – the most commonly used, expresses an unbridled, exuberant worship: *"My soul will **make its boast** in the LORD"* *(Psalm 34:2)*. Our English word "hallelujah" comes from a combination of this word and Yahweh/God.

BARAK – to kneel or bow and bless God: *"**Bless** the LORD, O my soul, And all that is within me, **bless** His holy name"* *(Psalm 103:1)*.

SHACHAH – bowing down before: the Israelites *"bowed low and **worshiped** the LORD with their faces to the ground"* *(Nehemiah 8:6)* and *"Come, let us **worship** and bow down"* *(Psalm 95:6)*.

YADAH – taken from two words that mean "to extend the hand" and "to God," either in adoration or surrender: *"My heart trusts in Him, and I am helped; Therefore my heart exults, And with my song I **shall thank** Him"* *(Psalm 28:7b)*.

ABAD – to do service or work for God: *"You shall fear only the LORD your God; and you* **shall worship** *Him"* (Deuteronomy 6:13) and *"***Worship** *the LORD with reverence"* (Psalm 2:11).

SHABACH – declare the glory of God to God: *"Because your lovingkindness is better than life, my lips* **will praise** *You"* (Psalm 63: 3).

The New Testament also uses several Greek words for worship. Two of the most commonly used are:

LATREUO – suggests rendering honor, or paying homage. *"I urge you therefore, brethren, by the mercies of God, to present your bodies a living and holy sacrifice, acceptable to God, which is your spiritual* **service of worship** *"* (Romans 12:1).

PROSKUNEO – literally means "to bow and kiss" in humble adoration: *"But an hour is coming, and now is, when the true* **worshipers** *shall* **worship** *the Father in spirit and truth; for such people the Father seeks to be His* **worshipers.** *God is spirit; and those who* **worship** *Him must* **worship** *in spirit and truth"* (John 4: 23-24).

I'll never forget when our pastor, Larry Kayser, taught on the meaning of *proskuneo* a number of years ago and challenged us with the question, "Are you getting close enough to God in your times with Him to bow and kiss Him?" I was incredibly challenged by that, and I try to make it my goal in my personal times of worship to not leave until I've been close enough to bow and kiss my Savior.

These Hebrew and Greek definitions show us that worship truly melds outward expressions with our most intimate attitudes toward God. We see expressions of exuberance, adoration, and surrender, as well as blessing, bowing, and serving. Warren Wiersbe said, "True worship is balanced and involves the mind, the emotions, and the will. Worship is personal and passionate, not formal and unfeeling, and it is our response to the living God, voluntarily offered to Him as He has offered Himself to us. . . . **Worship is the**

response of all that we are to all that God is and does" (emphasis mine).[2] I love that definition: " . . . ALL that we are to ALL that God is . . . " That consuming, selfless desire to give to God is the essence and the heart of worship. In the process, we are exposed to His holiness, His truth, His beauty, His love, and His purpose. We are exposed to His glory!

We shouldn't be surprised that the concept of worship dominates the Bible. The Bible establishes that God's priority always has been, and always will be, worship. Worship was His idea – His greatest passion. Before all of creation – before the earth was formed, before a single beast was created – worship was taking place. *"You alone are the LORD. You have made the heavens, the heaven of heavens with all their host, the earth and all that is on it, the seas and all that is in them. You give life to all of them and the heavenly host bows down before You"* (Nehemiah 9:6). The heavenly hosts were worshiping!

All of creation proclaims God's glory. *"The heavens are telling of the glory of God; and their expanse is declaring the work of His hands"* (Psalm 19:1). *"All you have made will praise you, O LORD; your saints will extol you"* (Psalm 145:10). When we look at all that His hands have made (as if we really could), we are struck by the greatness and majesty of our God. We're overwhelmed by how incomprehensible He truly is. And we struggle to see past our smallness and insignificance, to fathom just how infinitely valuable of a treasure we are to Him. As David expressed: *"O LORD, our Lord, How majestic is Your name in all the earth, Who have displayed Your splendor above the heavens! . . . When I consider Your heavens, the work of Your fingers, The moon and the stars, which You have ordained; What is man that You take thought of him, And the son of man that You care for him? Yet You have made him a little lower than God, And You crown him with glory and majesty!"* (Psalm 8:1,3-5).

Then God gave us the Ten Commandments, where he called for and regulated worship in the first two commands: *"You shall have no other gods before me. You shall not make for yourself an idol in the form of anything in heaven above or on the earth beneath or in the waters below. You shall not bow down to them or worship them; for I, the LORD your God, am a jealous God" (Exodus 20:3-5).* Throughout the Old Testament, it is clear that worship was very much the focus of many of God's people. In a song that Moses and the sons of Israel sang to the Lord, they sang, *"Who is like You among the gods, O LORD? Who is like You, majestic in holiness, Awesome in praises, working wonders?" (Exodus 15:11).* From the design of the Tabernacle, to the religious, social, and even political activity, to the significance of the burnt offerings, worship was constantly held up as the priority. More than that, it was an unswerving call to worship God wholly and unrestrained.

The magi were the first people to seek after Jesus, and their initial response was to worship. *"And they came into the house and saw the Child with Mary His mother; and they fell down and worshiped Him. Then, opening their treasures, they presented to Him gifts of gold, frankincense, and myrrh" (Matthew 2:11).* Actually, the first person to worship Jesus may have been prenatal John, leaping in his mom's womb at the presence of Jesus (Luke 1:39-45). Elizabeth knew immediately from her baby's response that Mary was carrying her Lord. The presence of Jesus is that powerful!

Throughout Jesus' earthly ministry, He drew people's worship wherever He went, often after the display of one of His many miracles. (Find examples in Matthew 14:22-33; Matthew 15:22-28; Mark 2:1-12; Luke 13:10-13; John 9:1-38.) But I believe my favorite is the story found only in Luke 7:36-50: *"And there was a woman in the city who was a sinner; and when she learned that He was reclining at the table in the Pharisee's house, she brought an alabaster vial of perfume, and standing behind Him at His feet, weeping, she began to wet His feet with her tears, and kept wiping them with the hair of her head, and kissing His feet and anointing them with the perfume" (v.37-38).* I imagine this to be Jesus' favorite picture of worship – the broken, repentant heart humbly bowing to its accepting, forgiving Savior. This is why He came, after all. Of course, the prideful Pharisee, Simon, couldn't understand why Jesus wouldn't just reject the display of that *"sort of person" (v.39)*. He couldn't grasp a forgiveness that's free to all who will receive it. And he couldn't respect the great lengths that she had gone to so that she could express her great sorrow for her sin, as well as her deep gratitude and love for her Savior. This is the picture of *proskuneo* worship that He longs for – sinners bowing and kissing their Deliverer.

After Christ's earthly ministry, Paul states the true mark of a believer, saying, *"for we are the true circumcision, who worship in the Spirit of God and glory in Christ Jesus and put no confidence in the flesh" (Philippians 3:3)*. Paul is making a statement (if you back up to v.2) against what was legal worship, consisting of rules regarding times, places, and outward acts. And he's calling for true Christian worship, which is a result of the inner working of the Holy Spirit in a person's life in response to the glory of Jesus. We should pray that we could see Jesus' glory as clearly as those who first saw Him in Mary's arms and be so driven to fall before Him in worship.

The book of Revelation so magnificently gives us a picture of what we expect in our eternity in heaven. Of the angels and the living creatures and the elders, it says, *"and the number of them was myriads of myriads, and thousands of thousands, saying with a loud voice, 'Worthy is the Lamb that was slain to receive power and riches and wisdom and might and honor and glory and blessing.' And every created thing which is in heaven and on the earth and under the earth and on the sea, and all things in them, I heard saying, 'To Him who sits on the throne, and to the Lamb, be blessing and honor and glory and dominion forever and ever'" (Revelation 5:11c-13)*. Wow! I believe we'll find eternity and worship to be synonymous. I'm sure there are no words to describe the overwhelming depth of love, and power, and awe that we will experience there, as we finally gaze in our heavenly state upon the God of all creation – the Savior of the World! Our compulsion to worship won't be denied, and we will never grow tired of it!

Our goal now is to consider what the Bible teaches us about worship, so we can understand what its call is for us today. Though the aim of this study is on those specific times set aside to put our focus on extending our worship to God, I need to make sure to emphasize that much, if not all, we do can be, and should be, acts of worship. Paul says in 1 Corinthians 10:31, " . . . *whatever you do, do all to the glory of God"* (emphasis mine). Then there's the command in 1 Corinthians 6:20: *"For you have been bought with a price; therefore glorify God in your body."* And what about Jesus' answer to the Pharisees' trick (so they thought) question: *"'Teacher, which is the great commandment in the Law?' And He said to him, 'You shall love the Lord your God with all your heart, and with all your soul, and with all your mind. This is the great and foremost commandment'"* (*Matthew 22:36-38,* emphasis mine).

I don't see any exceptions listed in those verses. I only see words like "whatever" (not the way it's said these days) and "all" used repeatedly. I don't see "unless," or "except," "if you'd like to," or even "if you feel like it." We're obviously being challenged to walk daily with an acute God-awareness, so we can glorify Him in *whatever* and in *all* we do. Those words are all-inclusive. That means that we can even glorify God while we're in the midst of our daily work routine: doing the laundry AGAIN, taking our daily jog, mowing the lawn, picking up groceries, dealing with the difficult co-worker or neighbor, carting the kids to their next event, or WHATEVER (apart from sin, of course). Dare I say that some may worship God more while doing those things than others do while sitting in church pews singing? (Ouch!)

In *Destined for the Throne,* Paul Billheimer writes, "To be most effective, then, praise must be massive, continuous, a fixed habit, a full-time occupation, a diligently pursued vocation, a total way of life. This principle is emphasized in Psalm 57:7: *'My heart is fixed, O God, my heart is fixed; I will sing and give praise.'* This suggests a premeditated and predetermined habit of praise, *'my heart is fixed.'"*[3] David wrote this psalm when he was running from Saul, so it was obviously not a time of being emotionally elated. It went far beyond his circumstances, because worshiping God was the pattern of his life.

Again, this does not happen accidentally. We each need to make the decision that we want to grow and develop the habit of walking in God-awareness, morning 'til night, striving to please and love Him in all respects. It means beginning each morning by giving yourself to God – body, mind, and soul – and inviting Him into your day. And it means allowing the Holy Spirit to draw us into an intimate relationship, attuned to His love-filled proddings and gentle corrections moment by moment. We have Jesus' promise in John 14:26: *"But the Helper, the Holy spirit, whom the Father will send in My name, He will teach you all things, and bring to your remembrance all that I said to you."* This is not something that God ever intended for us to do on our own power. But He needs our agreement, willingness, and diligence to seek and walk with Him whole-heartedly.

So if our whole life should be an act of worship to God, why do we also need to focus on specific times of offering worship to Him? Just as we're commanded to pray without ceasing (1 Thessalonians 5:17), we obviously also need times set aside for uninterrupted prayer, as Jesus modeled during His earthly life (Matthew 14:23). We'll see throughout this study that the same goes with our worship life. Plus, our times of focused worship serve as a catalyst for living a lifestyle of worship. Worship is a vital element for victorious Christian living, because the presence of God transforms us – compels us.

Join me on this important and transforming journey called worship. Let's see from the word of God what His intent and purpose regarding worship is for all of us. I promise you will never be the same. And it's how we'll return the crown jewel of evangelical Christianity – one worshiper at a time.

Pause: to reflect and pray

How am I doing when it comes to daily walking with acute God-awareness? What steps should I take to grow in that area?

How have these initial definitions and verses about worship opened my eyes to what God intends for me as His worshiper?

Is worship the priority that it should be in my life? Explain.

What am I hoping to gain from this study?

Write out a prayer asking God to open your heart and mind to better understand His call to you as His worshiper. (There are blank pages in the back of this study to provide additional writing space, if needed.)

PROFILES

It is good to give thanks to the LORD,
And to sing praises to Your name, O Most High;
to declare Your lovingkindness in the morning,
And Your faithfulness by night,
With the ten-stringed lute, and with the harp;
With resounding music upon the lyre.
For You, O LORD, have made me glad by what You have done,
I will sing for joy at the works of Your hands.

Psalm 92:1-4

Lesson Two

PROFILES in Worship

*W*hat *happened when people in the Bible worshiped?* My personal journey studying worship began with fervently seeking an answer to that question. These first two stories we'll look at were ones I had probably read or heard taught dozens of times, but my eyes were opened in a jaw-dropping way this time. What I learned could have huge implications for my life, if I let it. To take you on the same journey I was on, let's begin where I did, with Paul and Silas.

Note: I encourage you to look up any of the verses used throughout this study in your own Bible, both for gaining insight from different translations and for marking verses that impact you, so you can more easily return to them later.

Paul and Silas - Acts 16:16-33

Read verses 16-21: *"It happened that as we were going to the place of prayer, a slave-girl having a spirit of divination met us, who was bringing her masters much profit by fortune-telling. Following after Paul and us, she kept crying out, saying, 'These men are bond-servants of the Most High God, who are proclaiming to you the way of salvation.' She continued doing this for many days. But Paul was greatly annoyed, and* *turned and said to the spirit, 'I command you in the name of Jesus Christ to come out of her!' And it came out at that very moment. But when her masters saw that their hope of profit was gone, they seized Paul and Silas and dragged them into the market place before the authorities, and when they had brought them to the chief magistrates, they said, 'These men are throwing our city into confusion, being Jews, and are proclaiming customs which it is not lawful for us to accept or to observe, being Romans.'"*

This is one of many Biblical examples of followers of Christ being condemned for doing absolutely nothing wrong. Casting out the evil spirit that was plaguing this woman was obviously pleasing to God, and you'd think that men would be grateful, too. But their only focus was on losing the financial profit that they made from her terrible affliction. (It's interesting to note that the fortune-teller was saying nothing incorrect at this time, but it was still considered evil because of its source.)

Read verses 22-24 from your own Bible.

Paul and Silas are obviously now in physical pain, but what kinds of emotions might they be feeling at this point? Anxiety? Fear? Anger? How about hopelessness, discontentment, self-centered-ness, powerlessness, faithlessness, and a whole slew of other nega-tive responses that we could come up with? I don't think any of us would blame them for feeling any of these things, either. After all, they were human, just like us. What would I be feeling at this point, if I had been beaten and chained for simply doing what was right? (Unfortunately, this still happens in the world today.) More specifi-cally, what would I be feeling towards God?

Read verse 25.

What a truly amazing moment. This was not a response that came out of any of the probable emotions that we just listed. This was the response of men who knew, loved, and still trusted their God, in spite of their circumstances. This was the response of men who knew that their only source of strength in their weakness, and their only source of grace in their agony, was the God whom they worshiped with their whole hearts. We can only imagine the intense prayers that poured from their lips that night. But we know that their God was present and attentive, and that He ministered to their battered bodies, minds, and souls. And out of that place of much-needed grace came their heart-felt songs of praise to Him. Who was listening to this very unnatural response of worship that was loud enough to carry throughout the prison? The other prisoners undoubtedly heard, and maybe even saw, Paul and Silas being taken into the inner prison earlier. Can you imagine what they might have been thinking about this spontaneous midnight worship? I'm sure that their initial response was to think that the new prisoners had surely gone insane. But as they began to really *"listen"* (v.25), and not just hear, I imagine they quickly began to wonder *what* God can elicit such powerful words of praise and glory from such unexpected mouths. And *what* God can turn broken and beaten bodies into vessels full of such unbridled joy. Paul and Silas' worship was even more compelling, because they were probably singing one of David's psalms or hymns; and the Word of God always goes out with power!

Read verses 26-28.

Wow! What powerful results! Earthquakes were seen as evidence of the presence of God in response to His children's seeking of Him (such as in Acts 4:31). And the unfastening of everyone's chains would not be a result of your average earthquake. But why didn't Paul and Silas run? They were free! Honestly, that would've been my first reaction. But I think that there were several reasons. They absolutely believed that their God, who had already put on that great display of power for them, would continue to move on their behalf. Plus, I think that they wanted to both guarantee the jailer's safety and take advantage of the incredible audience they had with a bunch of awe-struck, fellow prisoners! So against all human inclinations, they stayed.

I believe there's more to this story, though. I believe that it's possible that the chains that dropped from Paul and Silas as a result of their worship were not *merely* the ones on their feet. But the chains of all of those difficult emotions that we listed a moment ago – chains of anxiety, fear, anger, hopelessness, and more – also fell. Their choice to worship is an example of how God can work in our hearts despite our circumstances and feelings. Both the physical and emotional chains dropping are an example of His power released in praise – a power that set them free in more than one way. What a great example of how our offering of praise and worship invites God to work and opens our hearts to His changing power.

Read verses 29-34.

The end result of Paul and Silas' faithfulness to turn to God in an attitude of worship was the powerful salvation story of the jailer and his family. After witnessing God's power in the earthquake, in the physical releasing of the chains, and in Paul and Silas' implausible attitudes, he asked, *"What must I do to be saved?" (v.30).* His heart turned from fighting, to keep them captive, to hungering to know their kind of freedom. He wanted to know their God. And he wanted to help these men who had just opened his eyes to true salvation. So Paul and Silas got the unforeseen opportunity to share Jesus with the jailer's entire family and to baptize them. Powerful.

(I encourage you to read the rest of Acts 16, as Paul and Silas chose to go back into the prison after their time with the jailer's family in the middle of the night. I love their courage and boldness!)

We face situations all the time that aren't nearly as difficult as this but that still bring us face to face with very similar emotions. What keeps us from choosing to worship God in each situation? I think it's because we struggle to take our eyes off of ourselves and what's going on around us, and we therefore fail to focus on God and seek His help. We let our chains, big and small, weigh us down, because we don't know or believe He can free us from them. I'm not saying

24

it's easy, or that God's response will always be this dramatic. But choosing to seek and worship God in the midst of those chain-bound moments invites His work, His presence, and His freedom. In our powerlessness, He is our strength. Worship can free us from life's chains as we put our focus on Him.

Though Paul and Silas' story is incredible and challenging enough, there's more! Keep reading!

King Jehoshaphat and the people of Judah
- 2 Chronicles 20: 1-24

Read verses 1-4: *"Now it came about after this that the sons of Moab and the sons of Ammon, together with some of the Meunites, came to make war against Jehoshaphat. Then some came and reported to Jehoshaphat, saying, 'A great multitude is coming against you from beyond the sea, out of Aram and behold, they are in Hazazon-tamar (that is Engedi).' Jehoshaphat was afraid and turned his attention to seek the LORD, and proclaimed a fast throughout all Judah. So Judah gathered together to seek help from the LORD; they even came from all the cities of Judah to seek the LORD."*

The first thing that Jehoshaphat did, upon hearing that this multitude was coming to make war against him, was to acknowledge his fear, seek God, and proclaim a fast throughout Judah. It's hard to not point out what most kings would have done – call together an army!

Read verses 5-13 from your own Bible.

I love how Jehoshaphat began his prayer by acknowledging who God was and proclaiming His power and might. He worshiped! He then continued his prayer by restating God's promises, recounting God's past faithfulness, and admitting his own powerlessness and lack of wisdom. He boldly proclaimed his trust in God, as he and

Judah sought the Lord together in this time of crisis. Many lessons for us there!

Read verses 14-19.

What a powerful message and response: "Do not fear. Trust Me." "We trust You. We worship You."

Read verses 20-24.

Receiving instructions like these and then following through with them are two very different things. They stepped out in faith and trusted God before any physical signs of the answer came. There would have been so many barriers to standing weaponless in front of a multitude of warriors like that: fear, faithlessness, helplessness. But Jehoshaphat reminded his people when they got there to put their trust in the Lord and succeed. And then the really cool part (to me)? He appointed singers and worshipers to go out in front before the army to declare the lovingkindness of the Lord! I find it interesting that they weren't singing about God's strength and might but about His *love*. His everlasting love. And then their enemies all dropped dead, destroying each other. Again, the power of faith-filled worship is exhibited in an amazing way.

This incredible story led me to ask myself several questions: *What if I worshiped God first in the midst of fear and tribulation? What if I was more diligent to acknowledge who God was as the first step in my battles? Am I missing out on seeing the power of being true worshiper? Could God be waiting to do things on my behalf that I miss out on, because I don't stop to acknowledge or worship Him first?*

It's my prayer that as this study progresses, we will learn more from people like Paul and Silas, as well as from Jehoshaphat and the people of Judah, that will help us to become more diligent, faith-filled worshipers.

Before we reflect on what we've just read, I need to make one more comment. Early in my study I shared some of my thoughts with Joe Horness, a friend, a gifted worship leader, and a teacher on worship. He warned against seeing worship as a consumer activity – as a way to get something out of God. God blesses us indeed when we worship, *but the focus of our worship needs to be remembering and exalting God for who He is* – period. Our worship's purpose is not seeking any resulting blessing, though God does graciously bless us. *He* is the focus. *He* is the purpose. His glory alone.

Pause: to reflect and pray

Considering Paul and Silas:
What chains, emotional or otherwise, are tying me down or keeping me from wanting to worship right now?

Considering King Jehoshaphat and the people of Judah:
Am I quick to seek and worship God in the difficult times of my life? Or do I struggle? Explain.

As a result of reading these two stories, what steps is God leading me to take in my worship life?

Ask God to help you see the importance of bringing Him into every area of your life. Ask Him to help you grow in your understanding and experience of worshiping Him as a way of life - in any circumstance of life.

Now spend some time in worship before Him.

Next: As I studied these stories, and many others in the Word, I felt compelled to continue to examine all that makes up this incredible thing we strive to do, called worship. The process took me down a road of distinguishing eight different facets of worship that we'll now look at individually. So *"may the eyes of your heart be enlightened" (Ephesians 1:18)* as you continue on this journey!

PERSON

Praise the LORD!
Praise the LORD, O my soul!
I will praise the LORD while I live;
I will sing praises to my God while I have my being.
How blessed is he whose help is the God of Jacob,
Whose hope is in the LORD his God,
Who made heaven and earth,
The sea and all that is in them;
Who keeps faith forever;
Who executes justice for the oppressed;
Who gives food to the hungry.
The LORD sets the prisoners free.
The LORD opens the eyes of the blind;
The LORD raises up those who are bowed down;
The LORD loves the righteous;
The LORD protects the strangers;
He supports the fatherless and the widow,
But He thwarts the way of the wicked.
The LORD will reign forever,
Your God, O Zion, to all generations.
Praise the LORD!

Psalm 146:1-2, 5-10

Lesson Three

The PERSON We Worship

Knowing the PERSON of God is crucial for true worship to happen.

It's essential. It's foundational. Without it our worship would be like a choir without a song or a Super Bowl without a football team. It is the crucial necessity of intimately knowing the person of God.

*"For I delight in loyalty rather than sacrifice, and in **knowledge of God** rather than burnt offerings" (Hosea 6:6).*

In Jesus' priestly prayer He said, *"And this is eternal life, that they may **know You**, the only true God, and Jesus Christ whom You have sent" (John 17:3).*

These verses elevate the knowledge of God to extreme importance. In fact, the Hebrew word *da'at*, translated as *"knowledge of God"* in Hosea 6:6, most accurately expresses an experiential knowledge. It's way beyond the mere acknowledgement that God simply exists, for even the demons acknowledge that (James 2:19). But it expresses a personal, intimate awareness of who God is and what He's done that results in an awe-inspired, complete, and utter devotion to Him.

If we could pray but one prayer, it should be that we would grow to know and love God more. When those two things are happening, all other aspects of the Christian life – such as prayer, obedience, serving, and giving – grow as a direct result. And that includes our worship life. True worship is grounded in the critical issue of knowing and loving God.

Here's the problem. There's a tendency to view God in human terms, as actually being no different from ourselves. Now no one will quickly agree that they do that. But how often do we consent with the voice in our head that whispers, "God can't (or wouldn't) do that" or "He doesn't really care (or listen)"? That list of doubts could go on and on. We sing the great songs, mouth the verses, and nod in agreement. But when it comes down to what we really, deeply believe, so many of us have little ambition to want to get to know, or especially bow in worship to, *that* God. In Psalm 50:21, God confronted those who didn't honor Him with, *"You thought that I was just like you."* So the question needs to be asked: Are we worshiping the God of the Bible who is *infinite* and *holy* – or a god that's limited by what our minds can grasp and our society can accept?

Psalm 145:3 says, *"Great is the LORD, and highly to be praised; And His greatness is unsearchable."*

And in Romans 11:33, 36 we read, *"Oh, the depth of the riches both of the wisdom and knowledge of God! How unsearchable are His judgments and unfathomable His ways! For from Him and through Him and to Him are all things. To Him be the glory forever. Amen."*

According to these verses, praise and glory belong to the unsearchable, unfathomable God! None of us will ever understand God perfectly on this side of heaven, for He cannot be limited by any kind of human definition. But we get into trouble when we try to make God too much like what we know and don't try to grow in the true knowledge of Him.

Proverbs 2:3-5 says, *"For if you cry for discernment, lift your voice for understanding; If you seek her as silver, and search for her as for hidden treasures; Then you will discern the fear of the LORD, and discover the knowledge of God"* (emphasis mine).

The writer of this proverb is describing an active pursuit of knowing and understanding God and the things of God. How active? Do we "cry," "lift our voice," "seek as silver," and "search as for a hidden treasure" in our quest to understand God?

Remember, Warren Wiersbe said, "Worship is the response of all that we are to *all that God is and does*" (emphasis mine).[1] We can't react to what we don't know. We can only worship God to the degree that we know Him. Otherwise, it's much like trying to go deep sea diving with a snorkel.[2] We've heard that so many amazing things lie in the vast waters far beyond what we can see. But if we're only willing to float on the surface of the water with a snorkel, then we can never truly experience or attempt to *know* that vastness. We settle for the shallowness. Yes, we can keep talking about that pretty orange, spotted fish that came up close, but that's not even a speck on the expanse of all that lies waiting to be revealed. And that ocean? Well, it's merely a speck on the vastness of all that is waiting to be revealed of God. After all, He created it – along with the rest of the universe. But unlike the ocean, God *longs* to reveal Himself to us. He relishes those times that we're willing to dive in headfirst and search with great expectancy for what He has for us next. Will it be the greater wonders of His love? His faithfulness? His power? His mercy? His holiness?

Worship leader Matt Redman says, "The *revelation of God* is the fuel for the fire of our worship" (emphasis mine).[3] If you remove the fuel to a fire, what happens? The fire goes out. But increase the fuel supply, which is the increased revelation of God, then the greater, and brighter, and more powerful, and more intimate the fire of our worship! It's in that place of focusing completely on *Him only* in worship, that we then finally see ourselves and our circumstances, in light of all that He is. And we can do nothing else in response but humbly bow in awe and worship.

The psalmist prayed, *"O send out Your light and Your truth, let them lead me; Let them bring me to Your holy hill and to Your dwelling places. Then I will go to the altar of God, to God my exceeding joy; And upon the lyre I shall praise You, O God, my God"* (Psalm 43:3-4). He's asking God to reveal Himself and that his response to that revelation would then be to worship.

The next question should then be - how do I get there? How do I "fuel the fire" of my worship? How do I dive in to truly search the depths of my unfathomable God?

Remember the conference I went to that motivated me to begin this study? If you remember, I said that each hour found me closer to the throne of God and with a clearer view of who He was. In other words, each time we worshiped, I found it easier to release those burdens, to forget what was going on around me and to focus less on me and more completely on God. I call it having *tunnel vision* for God. In high school, I had a friend named Al, who really had tunnel vision. His eyes quickly darted back and forth all of the time, trying to catch the whole picture in front of him, because he had no peripheral vision. He could only see where he was directly looking. God *wants* us to have tunnel vision for Him in our times of worship. He wants us to stop our minds from darting back and forth, so we can temporarily forget everything around us and see only Him. But that type of worship intimacy isn't going to happen in just 20 minutes every Sunday morning. We need to be seeking God throughout the week

So we're obviously not talking about mere head knowledge. We need to continually ask God to help us see Him more clearly and more fully; and we need to respond by pursuing a greater intimacy with the God who's revealing Himself to us. We do that by spending priority time with Him in the Word and in prayer. Only then will our relationship and heart knowledge of Him grow.

What's the key to seeking God? Two words:

Be still.

Be still. Stop. Let go. *"Cease striving and know that I am God"* (Psalm 46:10a).

We live in a society that no longer knows how to be still. But stillness is crucial for gaining knowledge and intimacy with God. It's crucial for calming the heart and mind. It's crucial for seeing, and it's crucial for truly hearing. We gain nothing with the drive-by glance mentality. Our heavenly Father is always calling us to Himself, saying, "Come to me. Be still and commune with My Spirit. Let Me pour out My love and grace over you. Come often. Stay long. Be still. I have so much for you here." And the second half of Psalm 46:10 shows the incredible results of being still. *"Cease striving and know that I am God. I will be exalted among the nations, I will be exalted in the earth"* (Psalm 46:10). Worship out of *that* place is the worship that God so longs for from us.

When it comes to times of personal worship, many find it helpful to have a list of the names of God and of His attributes as a prompt to remind us of who He is. If we had been able to eavesdrop and hear the words that Paul and Silas used in their worship of God in prison in the midst of their pain, fear, and powerlessness, I think we would've heard them worshiping those attributes about God that they most needed to see and experience. I think they would've been worshiping the God Who Sees, the God Who is in Control, the God Who is All-Powerful, the God Who Loves, and the God Who is Faithful! And remember how Jehoshaphat began his prayer to God as he stood before the people of Judah at such a fearful time? He said, *"O LORD, the God of our fathers, are You not God in the heavens? And are You not ruler over all the kingdoms of the nations?*

Power and might are in Your hand so that no one can stand against You" *(2 Chronicles 20:6).* He began by proclaiming and exalting who God was and continued by remembering what God had already done. No wonder their perspective on their situation was so incredibly affected when they chose to focus on, seek, and worship the incredible God that they undoubtedly knew so intimately!

There are many Biblical examples of those who chose to focus their attention on their glorious God. One of my favorites is David's prayer before all the assembly of Israel after they had all brought offerings for the temple that was to be built. David said, *"Yours, O LORD, is the greatness and the power and the glory and the victory and the majesty, indeed everything that is in the heavens and the earth; Yours is the dominion, O LORD, and You exalt Yourself as head over all. Both riches and honor come from You, and You rule over all, and in Your hand is power and might; and it lies in Your hand to make great and to strengthen everyone. Now therefore, our God, we thank You, and praise Your glorious name"* *(1 Chronicles 29:11-13). Then, after he finished his prayer, he said to the assembly, "'Now bless the Lord your God.' And all the assembly blessed the LORD, the God of their fathers, and bowed low and did homage to the Lord . . . "* *(v.20).*

"There's definitely a different dynamic in worship that kicks in when we fix our eyes firmly on Jesus," Matt Redman says. "I worry that too often we spend our worship times reflecting on how we are doing and what we have gained. As Anthony Bloom once said, 'So often when we say "I love you," we say it with a huge 'I' and a small 'you.' But there's a wonderful biblical dynamic in worship when we lift our eyes off ourselves and gaze upon the beauty of God."[4] That's when we're different when we come down off the mountain, like Moses in Exodus 34:29, "radiant for all to see, and shining with the glory of God."[5]

A line in one of Matt Redman's well-known worship songs, "Let Everything that Has Breath," expresses it well: "If we could see how much You're worth, Your power, Your might, Your endless love, surely we would never cease to praise You."[6] What a great line and how true!

Each glimpse – every breath-taking disclosure – is a divine gift that leaves us with the greater realization that there's still *so much more* to our Savior. It increases our passion to keep seeking Him. And though every glance is merely a drop in that vast ocean that's beckoning for our exploration, we need to keep nurturing that fascination with our unsearchable God. Our breath will then be taken away in worship.

Additional reading: Psalm 29:1-2; Psalm 103:1-5; Psalm 115:1

Pause: to reflect and pray

Do I struggle to fix my eyes firmly on Jesus or to have tunnel vision for Him during my times of worship? Explain.

How am I doing at seeking to know God more? Am I good at being still before Him?

What steps should I take to pursue growing to know and love God more intimately?

Included is a list of the names and titles of God to use in times of prayer and worship (see Appendix). Reading over them now, what characteristics about God or what names of God do I need to see moving in my life?

Write out in the form of worship the attributes/names of God that correspond to your current needs or desires.

Examples: In Psalm 27:1-3, when David was still surrounded by enemies, he said, *"The LORD is my light and my salvation; whom shall I fear? The LORD is the defense of my life; whom shall I dread? When evildoers came upon me to devour my flesh, my adversaries and my enemies, they stumbled and fell."* He's remembering who God is, as well as His past faithfulness.

Or for example: "Lord, you know that I feel completely incompetent at [*insert*]. But You are All-Powerful. When I am weak, You are strong. You are All-Wise and promise to give me wisdom when I ask. When I am faithless, You are Faithful. You are always good . . ."

Now write your own.

POSITION

O come, let us sing for joy to the LORD,
Let us shout joyfully to the rock of our salvation.
Let us come before His presence with thanksgiving,
Let us shout joyfully to Him with psalms.
For the LORD is a great God
and a great King above all gods,
In whose hand are the depths of the earth,
The peaks of the mountains are His also.
The sea is His, for it was He who made it,
And His hands formed the dry land.
Come, let us worship and bow down,
Let us kneel before the LORD our Maker.
For He is our God,
And we are the people of His pasture
and the sheep of His hand.

Psalm 95:1-7b

Lesson Four

Our POSITION in Worship

Worship begins with a heart prepared and POSITIONED to be fixed on God.

"My heart is fixed, O God, my heart is fixed; I will sing and give praise!" (Psalm 57:7,KJV)

"Who may ascend into the hill of the LORD? And who may stand in His holy place?" (Psalm 24:3)

We just can't go any further into the discussion on worship without seeking an answer to the question raised by David in Psalm 24. Does the Bible say who's allowed to enter the presence of the Most High God and stand before His throne? Does it assert who may offer worship or what makes a person's worship acceptable to Him? Very clearly.

The answer is given as Psalm 24 continues: *"He who has clean hands and a pure heart, Who has not lifted up his soul to falsehood and has not sworn deceitfully. He shall receive a blessing from the LORD and righteousness from the God of his salvation. This is the generation of those who seek Him, who seek Your face – even Jacob" (v.4-6).*

According to these verses, a worshiper must have *"clean hands"* (an obedient life before God) and *"a pure heart"* (right motives and desires before God), *"not lifted up his soul to falsehood"* (a truth-centered life), or *"not sworn deceitfully"* (no unkept promises).

It's pretty clear here that worship is not an event or practice that can be separated in the least from the rest of a person's life. If we choose to live a life that is contrary to God's word, then any words of worship we may mouth at church, or anywhere else, fall empty. Those blemished offerings don't even make it to *"His holy place"* *(v.3)*. That's because sin draws us away from God and away from true worship. But it's also because a Holy God cannot be in the presence of sin. Isaiah 59:2 says, *"But your iniquities have made a separation between you and your God, And your sins have hidden His face from you so that He does not hear."* But He hasn't left us in this hopeless situation. We have a choice. Let's keep looking.

Hebrews 10:19, 22 gives rich insight into what kind of preparation God expects from His worshipers: *"Therefore, brethren, since we have confidence to enter the holy place by the blood of Jesus . . . [Then] Let us draw near with a sincere heart in full assurance of faith, having our hearts sprinkled clean from an evil conscience and our bodies washed with pure water."*

Again, here's a verse that gives us four conditions necessary to be ready to *"enter the holy place"* or a place of worship. The first is having a *"sincere heart."* We need to have hearts that are truly fixed on God, not self-absorbed, hypocritical, preoccupied, or apathetic. Second, we need to draw near *"in full assurance of faith."* The worshiper needs to come to God fully assured that his access is by faith alone in Jesus Christ. The third condition listed here is *"having hearts sprinkled clean."* We must come knowing that we only have the right to be there because we've been cleansed by the blood of Jesus. And finally, we come with *"our bodies washed with pure water."* I believe this refers to the necessary daily confession of sin – just as 1 John 1:9 refers to God's faithfulness to *"cleanse us from all unrighteousness"* as we confess our sin. If we fulfill these four conditions, we will have every *"confidence"* to enter His presence and worship.

So what if you desire to *"enter the holy place"* to worship, and upon coming, realize that you don't have clean hands or a pure, sincere heart? The first step is to agree with God about the sin that He's showing you. Call the sin what it is and repent, which involves a change in attitude and action. Sincerely pray and ask God to forgive and cleanse you of the sin, thank Him for His promised forgiveness, and ask Him to empower you through His Spirit to walk in a way pleasing to Him. True worship involves a surrender and submission of everything we are before God.

It's so important to remember how we are even allowed to enter the holy presence of the Lord God Almighty to begin with. *"But as for me, by Your abundant lovingkindness I will enter Your house, At Your holy temple I will bow in reverence for You" (Psalm 5:7)*. It's only out of His *"abundant lovingkindness"* that we're ushered into His presence. He longs for us to be there. It was out of His abundant love that He offered His son, Jesus, to die on the cross for our sins, so that we might have access to Him by grace through faith (Ephesians 2:8). His love draws us. His love allows us. His love fills us. It's out of His undeserved love and grace that we have anything to offer back to Him in worship. And it's out of this love that He yearns for us to be His intimate worshipers.

There's obviously no hint of pride in true worship. Revelation 4:10-11 tells us that the 24 elders will cast their crowns before the throne in worship. Their crowns represent their greatest achievements on this earth. But everything they have to offer God on that day, even their crowns, comes from Him to begin with. Everything that we could possibly have to offer Him on that day, or every day before, comes from Him. What an amazing privilege that He fills us up with the riches of His glory, so that we might humbly bow before Him and pour it all back out at His feet. Worshiping our

God with all that we are and all that we have is acknowledging His inexplicable greatness and our utter dependency.

Carol Wimber said, "What happens when we are alone with the Lord determines how intimate and deep worship will be when we come together."[1] Can you even imagine a room full of people who were truly, scripturally ready to worship coming before His throne together? Wow!

Look at the words to this older, familiar worship chorus, "I Love You, Lord"[2]:

> *I love You, Lord*
> *And I lift my voice to worship You*
> *Oh, my soul rejoice*
> *Take joy my King in what You hear*
> *May it be a sweet, sweet sound in Your ear*

Considering this song, Gary Best said, "We assume that what we're singing must be a sweet, sweet sound to His ear. After all, the band is tight, our arms are raised. The angels must be taking the night off just to listen. But truthfully, not everything we sing and communicate, no matter how exhilarating the experience, or how enthusiastic the band, is a sweet sound in God's ear. You can fool all the people some of the time, and some of the people all the time . . . but you can't fool God any of the time. He looks past the words, the arms raised, the music, and sees the heart."[3]

Let's consider some more verses. These first three passages reiterate God's focus on the position of the heart of His worshiper.

"Then the Lord said, ' . . . this people draw near with their words and honor Me with their lip service, But they remove their hearts far from Me, and their reverence for Me consists of tradition learned by rote" (Isaiah 29:13). See also Jesus' quote from Isaiah in Matthew 15:8-9.

"And He said to them, 'Rightly did Isaiah prophesy of you hypocrites, as it is written: This people honors Me with their lips, but their heart is far away from Me. But in vain do they worship Me" (Mark 7: 6-7a).

"O Lord, open my lips, that my mouth may declare Your praise. For You do not delight in sacrifice, otherwise I would give it; You are not pleased with burnt offering. The sacrifices of God are a broken spirit; a broken and a contrite heart, O God, You wilt not despise" (Psalm 51:15-17).

" . . . we are the true circumcision, who worship in the Spirit of God and glory in Christ Jesus and put no confidence in the flesh" (Philippians 3:3). Our dependence on the Holy Spirit is the key to authentic worship.

"And Samuel said, 'Has the LORD as much delight in burnt offerings and sacrifices as in obeying the voice of the LORD? Behold, to obey is better than sacrifice, and to heed than the fat of rams" (1 Samuel 15:22). In Old Testament times, burnt offerings and sacrifices were an act of worship. But Samuel said the Lord's delight was in their hearts' attitude toward Him.

"And He looked up and saw the rich putting their gifts into the treasury. And He saw a certain poor widow putting in two small copper coins. And He said, 'Truly I say to you, this poor widow put in more than all of them; for they all out of their surplus put into the offering but she out of her poverty put in all that she had to live on'" (Luke 21:1-4). The widow's private, inconspicuous part of worship is what caught Jesus' eye. Matt Redman said, "God first seeks devotion to Him in the hidden place - worship when no one else is watching."[4]

"But an hour is coming, and now is, when the true worshipers will worship the Father in spirit and truth; for such people the Father seeks to be His worshipers. God is spirit, and those who worship him must worship in spirit and truth" (John 4:23-24). I like A.W. Tozer's frankness when he says, "Men and women continue to try to persuade themselves that there are many forms and ways that seem right in worship . . .

God takes the matter of worship out of the hands of men and puts it in the hands of the Holy Spirit . . . When a person, yielding to God and believing the truth of God, is filled with the Spirit of God, even his faintest whisper will be worship."[5] I love that.

This all leads us to ask: Are too few experiencing the kind of worship that God intended? Absolutely. So is this an insurmountable barrier? Absolutely NOT! True worship, just like the victorious Christian life, is the fruit of daily seeking to live in the power of the Holy Spirit. Just as we received Christ by faith, faith is the only means by which we can live the Spirit-filled life.[6] It's not something that God ever intended that we do on our own. There is an unlimited supply of grace and power to live the Christian life available to us at all times! Even though it's the enemy's greatest desire to defeat us every step of the way, our God is a God of incredible grace!

I'd like to offer one final ingredient necessary for our heart to be rightly positioned before God: thankfulness. *"Enter His gates with thanksgiving and [then] His courts with praise. Give thanks to Him, bless His name. For the LORD is good; His lovingkindness is everlasting and His faithfulness to all generations" (Psalm 100:4-5).* You have to go through the gate to get to the courts. I believe that we sometimes miss out on intimacy with God in His courts, simply because we're not thankful enough to get through the gate. It's important to God. We need to approach His throne remembering and being thankful for His goodness, His lovingkindness, and His faithfulness. We get the same encouragement from Psalm 95:2-3a: *"Let us come before His presence with thanksgiving, let us shout joyfully to Him with psalms. For the LORD is a great God . . . "*

Paul prayed for the believers in Ephesus, *"I pray that the eyes of your heart may be enlightened, so that you may know what is the hope of His calling, what are the riches of the glory of His inheritance in the saints, and what is the surpassing greatness of His power toward us who believe" (Ephesians 1:18-19).* So if you truly pray, "open the eyes of my heart," watch out! You may become the recipient of not only great knowledge and power of God, but of unfathomable worship!

Pause: to reflect and pray

What are some new insights on worship that I gained from the passages used here?

How will those insights impact how I approach worship in the future?

Looking back over the verses in this lesson, is the Holy Spirit showing me any areas of my life that are preventing me from intimately walking with and worshiping God? Be specific.

Thinking back over all of the lessons up to now, write out a prayer, asking God to continue to show you how to become the worshiper He intended you to be. Be still. Be quiet. Pour out your heart before Him. And write down anything you feel He is saying back to you.

Now spend some time in worship before Him.

PURPOSE

Yours, O LORD, is the greatness
and the power and the glory
and the victory and the majesty,
indeed everything that is in the heavens and the earth;
Yours is the dominion, O LORD,
and You exalt Yourself as head over all.
Both riches and honor come from You, and You rule over all,
and in Your hand is power and might;
and it lies in Your hand to make great and to strengthen everyone.
Now therefore, our God, we thank You,
and praise Your glorious name.

1 Chronicles 29:11-13

Lesson Five

The PURPOSE for Worship

Worship is God's **PURPOSE** for His seeking and saving us.

Worship isn't optional. Paul wrote in Philippians 2:9-11: *"**For this reason** also, God highly exalted Him, and bestowed on Him the name which is above every name, **so that** at the name of Jesus EVERY KNEE WILL BOW, of those who are in heaven and on earth and under the earth, and that every tongue will confess that Jesus Christ is Lord, to the glory of God the Father"* (emphasis mine).

During His temptation in Matthew 4:8-10, Jesus quoted Deuteronomy 6:13, saying, *"YOU SHALL WORSHIP THE LORD YOUR GOD, AND SERVE HIM ONLY."* And Jesus said to the woman at the well, *"But an hour is coming, and now is, when the true worshipers will worship the Father in spirit and truth; for such people the Father **seeks** to be His worshipers"* (John 4:23).

According to these verses, God sent us Jesus so that we would worship Him. And God diligently seeks after *us* so that we will worship Him. It's not something we throw into a church service just because it's always been done that way. God is deeply passionate about us being His worshipers!

So then, what is *our* purpose in worship? Remember the way that Warren Wiersbe stated it so purely and simply? "Worship is the response of all that we are to all that God is and does."[1] That reaction to who God *is* is expressed in three different elements: obedience, exaltation, and adoration. Let's look at each of these separately.

1) Obedience needs to be our first response to God's *command* to worship Him. This takes us right back to Matthew 4:10: *"YOU SHALL WORSHIP THE LORD YOUR GOD, AND SERVE HIM ONLY."* It seems like we shouldn't need to be commanded to worship God. When we look at Him in all His glory, power, and love, worship should be our natural response. But He commands us to, because He knows our weaknesses. He knows how easy it is for us to take our eyes off of Him – to get distracted and forget who He is. He also knows that the enemy tries his best to defeat us in this area. But what may at times begin as an act of obedience can turn into a heartfelt time of exaltation and adoration, if we're sincerely and rightly focusing on Him.

Remember Jesus' answer to what the greatest commandment was? *"YOU SHALL LOVE THE LORD YOUR GOD WITH ALL YOUR HEART, AND WITH ALL YOUR SOUL, AND WITH ALL YOUR MIND"* (Matthew 22:37). Loving God is demonstrated in many ways, but it begins with and is sustained by our obedience in worship.

2) Exaltation of God fulfills His purpose in creating us. When we exalt God, we lift Him to His proper place and acknowledge that He is God and we are not! William Temple said, " . . . to worship is to quicken the conscience by the holiness of God, to feed the mind with the truth of God, to purge the imagination by the beauty of God, to open the heart to the love of God, and to devote the will to the purpose of God."[2] It's all-encompassing. And when we lift Him to His proper place, we should naturally find our proper place, and then humbly bow at His feet, as the center of our focus is taken off of ourselves and put on our infinite God.

"Praise the Lord! Praise God in His sanctuary; Praise Him in His mighty expanse. Praise Him for His mighty deeds; Praise Him according to His excellent greatness" *(Psalm 150:1-3).*

*"Everyone who is called by My name, and whom I have created for **My glory"*** *(Isaiah 43:7).*

*"But you are a chosen race, a royal priesthood, a holy nation, a people for God's own possession, **so that** you may proclaim the excellencies of Him who has called you out of darkness into His marvelous light"* *(1Peter 2:9).*

Exaltation means to increase, to exalt above, to lift up high, to ascribe glory, to rejoice!

Every morning I use a 10x magnification mirror as I put on my makeup, so I can actually see what I'm doing. And I admit that I have a hard time not focusing on my self-perceived flaws when I see them so large. But when we *magnify* the Lord, it has the opposite effect. We see an even more marvelous picture of His true greatness, holiness, and glory. And the amazing truth is that God created us in His image (Genesis 1:26) so that we could reflect His glory. *"And we, who with unveiled faces all reflect the Lord's glory, are being transformed into his likeness with ever-increasing glory, which comes from the Lord, who is the Spirit"* *(2 Corinthians 3:18, NIV).* Our Heavenly Father longs for us to embrace His purpose for us as the magnifiers and exalters of the One True God!

3) Adoration is our *heart's* response of love and devotion in worship to our mind and voice's proclamation of the truth of who God is. It's a very important part of our worship experience. We were created to be worshipers. John Wimber said, "Our heart's desire should be to worship God; we have been designed by God for this purpose. If we don't worship God, we'll worship something or someone else."[3] We need to be seeking to know God so intimately that we store up an abundance of love for Him, out of which we pour out our adoration towards Him in worship. In Luke 6:45, Jesus says that the *"mouth speaks from that which fills his heart."* We don't merely lift our voices and hands when we worship; we must first lift our hearts.

"O God, You are my God; I shall seek You earnestly; My soul thirsts for You, my flesh yearns for You, In a dry and weary land where there is no water. Thus I have seen You in the sanctuary, To see Your power and Your glory. Because Your lovingkindness is better than life, My lips will praise You. So I will bless You as long as I live; I will lift up my hands in Your name. My soul is satisfied as with marrow and fatness, And my mouth offers praises with joyful lips" (Psalm 63:1-5). This is David's adoring response of who God is to him at a very difficult time in his life. God isn't just some mighty but distant God to David. God is *his* God. "You are *my* God," he exclaimed. He was basically saying, "Not only have I seen Your power and glory, and tasted Your lovingkindness, but *You are mine*. And what You have to offer me is far better than *all* of life. I *will* praise You forever." David *adored* God. Oh, how we should each pray that our hearts would be open and free to respond to our loving God with adoring worship!

What's the alternative to living a life of obediently exalting and adoring God? Living a life that only exalts one's own lostness. Paul described one such group of people in Romans 1:25 when he said, *"For they exchanged the truth of God for a lie, and worshiped and served the creature rather than the Creator, who is blessed forever."* Satan knows we are worshipers. So he deceives anyone who will listen, whispering twisted lies in our ears about who or what deserves that worship.

"Not to us, O LORD, not to us but to your name be the glory, because of your love and faithfulness. Why do the nations say, 'Where is their God?' Our God is in heaven; he does whatever pleases him. But their

idols are silver and gold, made by the hands of men. They have mouths, but cannot speak, eyes, but they cannot see; they have ears, but cannot hear, noses, but they cannot smell; they have hands, but cannot feel, feet, but they cannot walk; nor can they utter a sound with their throats. Those who make them will be like them, and so will all who trust in them" (Psalm 115:1-8).

It's staggering to what depths we'll sink to give so much glory to such unworthy recipients and for such empty results. How do we know where we stand as worshipers? Louie Giglio says, "It's easy. You simply follow the trail of your time, your affection, your energy, your money, and your allegiance. At the end of that trail you'll find a throne; and whatever, or whomever, is on that throne is what's of highest value to you. On that throne is what you worship."[4] That's a trail we all must follow on a regular basis to keep our worship life in check.

By the way, our heavenly Father loves us lavishly and relentlessly. Your heavenly Father loves **you** lavishly and relentlessly. He doesn't hold back. The cross is proof of that! And Zephaniah 3:17 says, *"He will exult over you with joy, He will be quiet in His love, He will rejoice over you with shouts of joy."* The Hebrew for *rejoice* in that verse literally means to "spin around with intense motion." If He so willingly lavishes His unconditional love on us, His imperfect and often unlovable children, then shouldn't we all the more be willing to express our love to our always loving, gracious, merciful, and faithful Father in return?

Matt Redman says of 2 Samuel 6:12-22, that King David "led the way, losing himself so publicly in his worship of God, and so on fire with praise that it burned right through any inhibitions of pride. True worship always forgets itself."[5] One of the Hebrew words for praise, *hallal*, means to be clamorously foolish or mad before the Lord. In Luke 7:36-50, the Pharisee didn't understand why Jesus allowed the woman, who was a sinner, to anoint Him with perfume. But the abundance of love and worship she was expressing was coming out a heart that had received an abundance of forgiveness. May *we* be that moved by the depths of forgiveness that God has lavished on us! Matt Redman also said, in relating this story of King David, "I sometimes find myself rationing out the oil of love for God, drop by drop, with no passion or spontaneity . . . A relationship with the living God shouldn't just fade away or wear out like an old pair of shoes. It's meant to be new every morning, just like the mercy it responds to."[6] We need to learn to freely respond to the God who so willingly reveals Himself and His love to us, just like the woman with her perfume – or even like King David! Or sometimes that may take the form of just needing to respond with simple quietness and stillness before Him – to sit and reflect with awe on who He is – and know that, yes, He is God (Psalm 46:10).

"For who in the skies is comparable to the LORD? Who among the sons of the mighty is like the LORD, a God greatly feared in the council of the holy ones, and awesome above all those who are around Him? O LORD God of hosts, who is like You, O mighty LORD?" (Psalm 89:6-8a).

"Then Moses said, 'I pray You, show me Your glory!'" (Exodus 33:18).

Again, we must never stop seeking to know more of God. We will only get a glimpse at a time in this life, but glimpse we must! For we must never forget that it's not about us. It's always about Him. And each glimpse of His glory changes us. And it increases our passion to humbly fulfill our greatest purpose and His highest desire as a most honored worshiper of the Almighty God.

Additional reading: Exodus 20:3; Psalm 99:9; Psalm 150

Pause: to reflect and pray

Is worshiping God an optional part of my life? Explain.

How am I doing at responding with obedience, exaltation, and adoration to God in worship?

Do I love God passionately enough to want to express it to Him through adoration in worship? What can I do to nurture that love?

Where does my worship trail lead? (The trail of your time, affection, energy, money, and allegiance.)

In what areas do I feel God is leading me to grow from this lesson?

Write out a prayer asking God to help you learn how to become the worshiper that He purposely created you to be. Ask Him to give you some specific steps to take to grow in the right direction. And worship Him.

PRESENCE

The LORD reigns, let the earth rejoice;
Let the many islands be glad.
Clouds and thick darkness surround Him;
Righteousness and justice are the foundation of His throne.
Fire goes before Him and burns up His adversaries round about.
His lightnings lit up the world;
The earth saw and trembled.
The mountains melted like wax at the presence of the LORD,
At the presence of the Lord of the whole earth.
The heavens declare His righteousness,
And all the peoples have seen His glory.

Psalm 97:1-6

Lesson Six

God's PRESENCE in Worship

The Bible's call for us to be worshipers is a call to bask in the amazing PRESENCE of God.

God wants us to *expect* to engage with Him closely as we lift up our hearts and minds in response to all that He is. 2 Chronicles 15:2 says, " . . . *the LORD is with you when you are with Him. And if you seek Him, He will let you find Him.*" You see, the Bible reveals a God who is constantly inviting us into His presence to worship Him. He *wants* to be seen by His children. He *longs* for us to know Him intimately. He knows that as we enter the temple of His presence in worship, that with each glimpse of His glory and every moment of awesome revelation, He'll gain a little more of our hearts. And He knows that our passion to come back for more grows as our picture of Him grows. (Remember Lesson 3.) Gradually we realize that with each of those glimpses, there is so much more to our God than we could ever imagine. And the most humbling of those discoveries is that the God who created the heavens and the earth actually does love us deeply and long to encounter us closely. We shouldn't ever cease to be amazed at those overwhelming truths. The Word's call to us is simple: *"Draw near to God and He will draw near to you" (James 4:8a).*

Yet how many of us enter our times of worship expecting nothing of the sort from God? Maybe He feels far away, or maybe the mystery is just too great, and we honestly do doubt His presence. The truth is that if you are a believer in Christ, then " . . . *He Himself has said, 'I will never desert you, nor will I ever forsake you'"* *(Hebrews 13:5b).* As a matter of fact, the reason we don't have to go to the temple to worship anymore, as in Old Testament times, is because we *each* are now the temple. He indwells us as believers in the person of the Holy Spirit. As 1 Corinthians 3:16 says, *"Do you not know that you are a temple of God and that the Spirit of God dwells in you?"* So you are a temple. I am a temple. We are living, breathing, skin-clad temples! And we can *expect* intimacy in worship with the God who lives in us. These are the moments that He truly longs for – when we turn and engage with Him with all our being. He's already right there waiting. We don't have to worship God from a distance! John Wimber said, "We should always come to worship prepared for an audience with the King."[1] I love that!

So what does it mean to bask in the presence of God? When I hear the word *bask,* I think of sun-worshipers. Anyone who has been to the beach has seen more sun-worshipers than necessary. And what do they do? They go to a place where the sun is the most intense. They then remove anything that hinders the sun's rays from desired contact, and just lie there . . . and lie there . . . and lie there. For they know that the longer they stay laid bare to the sun's influence, the greater the effect. Why are they called worshipers? Because taking in the sun is their primary goal while they're there. And true sun-worshipers keep going back, because they love the sun and want to keep those powerful effects.

How does that relate to us? We need regular times when we go to a place where we have undistracted contact with God – when seeing Him and worshiping Him is our only goal. (Back to tunnel vision!) We then need to remove anything that hinders His influence on our hearts, minds, and souls. That may be sin in our lives or personal burdens. Whatever it is, we need to take it off and lay it before Him to allow Him to work. And we also need times when we aren't clock watching and can just stay there to take in as much of His glory as

He'll share. We should be so enthralled with the awesomeness of God that we don't even notice the time or whether we've sung that chorus three times already! We only know that God is right there communing with us, and it's amazing. Our natural response will be to give back to Him all that He deserves from all we that are in the form of worship. It's a small taste of heaven, where all the distractions to our worship will finally be gone for good!

Of course, the comparison falls apart at one point. Most people know that too much contact with the earth's sun causes damage to our skin. But it's impossible to have too much contact with God's Son! We need to stay long, and we need to keep going back to keep His picture fresh and His influence real. Know that the greater depths of intimacy in worship won't come if all we ever have to offer God are "quickies." It will be in those times that we truly bask, or linger, that we'll feel the rewards of Him drawing us closer and maybe even revealing a little more of Himself to us. He never passively receives the time we spend focusing on Him. The "you reap what you sow" principle (as in Galatians 6:7-8) applies beautifully. Sow devoted time in your worship of God, and reap greater and greater rewards of His intimacy and joy. And the more frequently we make those lingering times of worship a priority, the more quickly He'll allow us to get to that place of intimacy with Him the next time. He truly relishes these times with us. And who knows – maybe we could come away like Moses in Exodus 34:29-35, with a God-tan!

Let's look in the Bible and see what the response is of someone who had truly basked in the presence of God.

*"¹How lovely are **Your dwelling places**, O LORD of hosts! ²My soul longed and even yearned for **the courts** of the LORD; My heart and my flesh sing for joy to the living God. ³The bird also has found a house, And the swallow a nest for herself, where she may lay her young, Even Your altars, O LORD of hosts, My King and my God. ⁴How blessed are those*

*who dwell in **Your house**! They are ever praising You. . . . [8]O Lord God of hosts, hear my prayer; Give ear, O God of Jacob! [9]Behold our shield, O God, And look upon the face of Your anointed. [10]For a day in **Your courts** is better than a thousand outside. I would rather stand at the threshold of **the house of my God** than dwell in the tents of wickedness. [11]For the LORD God is a sun and shield; The LORD gives grace and glory; No good thing does He withhold from those who walk uprightly. [12]O LORD of hosts, How blessed is the man who trusts in You!" (Psalm 84: 1-4; 8-12).*

The psalmist is expressing an intense longing and yearning to return to the presence of God (v.2). It was a place where he experienced complete satisfaction, joy, and peace that went far beyond casual church ritual. His whole being (*"heart and flesh," v.2*) is intensely longing to be back in that place of intimate fellowship with God, so much so, that if he had to choose, he'd settle for a mere glimpse of God's glory for a day, instead of being able to live for a thousand days apart from Him (v.10). It's a place that he receives all that's good and all that's needed (v.11). And I'm sure that even these words failed to express even a fraction of the passion that he was experiencing.

Let's look at some additional passages and see what we can glean about the Biblical writers' thoughts and feelings about God's presence in their worship.

*"O God, You are my God; I shall seek You earnestly; My soul thirsts for You, my flesh yearns for You, In a dry and weary land where there is no water. Thus **I have seen You in the sanctuary**, To see Your power and Your glory. Because Your lovingkindness is better than life, My lips will praise You. So I will bless You as long as I live; I will lift up my hands in Your name. My soul is satisfied as with marrow and fatness, And my mouth offers praises with joyful lips" (Psalm 63:1-5).*

*" . . . You make him (the king) most blessed forever; You make Him joyful with gladness **in Your presence**. For the king trusts in the Lord, And through the lovingkindness of the Most High he will not be shaken. Be*

exalted, O LORD, in Your strength; We will sing and praise Your power" (Psalm 21:6-7, 13).

*"Why are you in despair, O my soul? And why have you become disturbed within me? Hope in God, for I shall again praise Him for the help of **His presence**"* (Psalm 42:5).

*"Now to Him who is able to keep you from stumbling, and to make you **stand in the presence of His glory** blameless with great joy, to the only God our Savior, through Jesus Christ our Lord, be glory, majesty, dominion and authority, before all time and now and forever. Amen"* (Jude 1:24-25).

In each of these Psalms, the writers either sought or expected God's presence in their worship, or they worshiped as result of experiencing God's presence. The psalmists recognized His glory, His hand, and His movement in their lives in marvelous ways. His presence changed their very lives!

*"How blessed is the one whom You choose and **bring near to You**, To dwell in Your courts. We will be satisfied with the goodness of Your house, Your holy temple"* (Psalm 65:4).

I must admit that as unqualified, unworthy, inept, or (pick a word!) that I feel writing this entire study, that inability (and spiritual battle) is multiplied many times over in the writing of this particular chapter. How in the world do I explain something so incredible, yet so indescribable – so overwhelming, yet so humbling? There are no words that can express the depth of God's desire for us to experience His presence, any more than they can express the depths of God Himself. I just know that the God who sings and dances over us must relish and rejoice in those moments that we stop and pour out His praises and our adoration, straining along the way to get past the world so we can catch a glimpse of His glory. I'm not talking about working up a bunch of feelings, though they will come at times more strongly than others. I'm talking about seeking and responding rightly to the truth of who God is in that place where He's *waiting* to commune and reveal Himself a little more each time. The thought of it leaves me speechless. But He is faithful. He is gracious. And He will honor those who seek to be His worshipers with a clearer picture of Himself and greater taste of His presence. There is no greater privilege in this life!

"O taste and see that the LORD is good" (Psalm 34:8).

"Cease striving and know that I am God; I will be exalted among the nations, I will be exalted in the earth" (Psalm 46:10).

Pause: to reflect and pray

What are my thoughts as I read the intimate contemplations and prayers of the psalmists?

How do I anticipate connecting with God as I enter worship? Do I expect to engage with His presence closely - or do I struggle to *"draw near to God"*?

Do words like "yearn," "long," or "thirst" ever describe my desires toward seeking God's presence? When?

What words would best describe my worship experience - both privately and with others?

Is there anything in my life (e.g. sin, distraction, burden) hindering me from entering and experiencing God's presence in worship? Be specific. Have I confessed it to God or laid it before Him to allow Him to work?

What steps can I take to seek more focused time basking in the presence of God in worship?

Pray that God would increase your desire to seek His presence in worship, and that He'd help you understand His own desires for you in this area. Ask Him to reveal any hindrances keeping you from entering and experiencing His presence in worship. Seek His help to follow though on the steps you just listed. And finally, ask God to help you see Him more clearly as you position yourself to enter His presence to worship.

Now bow your heart before God to worship Him and seek His presence.

POWER

Shout joyfully to God, all the earth;
Sing the glory of His name;
Make His praise glorious.
Say to God, How awesome are Your works!
Because of the greatness of Your power
Your enemies will give feigned obedience to You.
All the earth will worship You,
And will sing praises to You;
They will sing praises to Your name.

Psalm 66:1-4

Lesson Seven

The POWER of Worship

God unleashes amazing **POWER** in response to His children's worship.

Attempting to uncover the power of worship that lies so descriptively within the pages of the Bible is not only challenging, but overwhelming and humbling as well. For I know full well that, as with the topics before this, there is much that's unexplainable and incomprehensible while in our earthly dwelling – like that which is miraculously unleashed when we freely lift the name of our Holy and Mighty God and responsively bow and kiss His feet. So though it may only be a scratch on the surface of the reality of what God does in response to the worship of His children, we must attempt it. For examining worship in God's Word reveals much of our Father's heart towards us, as we see His response to the worship that He's created us for.

Before I go on I need to reiterate that we do not enter worship in order to receive the blessing of God's power in our lives. He is God, and *we worship Him for who He is to us, **not** what He'll do for us*. It's not a consumer activity that says, "I give so I can receive." But it's one of selflessly giving ourselves to the God who selflessly gave Himself for us.

Now on to the topic at hand!

The worshiper who strives to live a life that truly glorifies and honors God will uncover an inexhaustible resource of power and purpose that God reserves for His true worshipers. " . . . *for those who honor Me I will honor"* (1 Samuel 2:30). This resource of power is gloriously displayed throughout the scriptures in both somewhat anticipated ways and in quite extraordinary moments. We've already looked at what I feel is the most amazing display of His power in worship – the experience of our Savior's presence. But the Old and New Testaments are full of examples of God honoring those who worshiped Him with various expressions of His power.

True worship is always transforming. When believers encounter God in genuine worship, He brings about transforming results from the inside out. These changes are, at the very core, a pouring out of our Heavenly Father's wondrous grace on us through the power of His Holy Spirit. While the external results should be apparent, the visible is merely an outward sign of His most important life-changing work deep inside in response to our worship.

Let's look, in no particular order, at the evidence of some of God's power-filled, transforming works in response to Bible-time worshipers.

1) Perspective – Change in perspective is one of those transforming works that results from true worship. **Take a moment now to read Psalm 8 and Psalm 73 from your Bible.**

These are just two of many great Biblical examples of the change in perspective brought about when people bowed their hearts and minds before God. We read in Psalm 8 that as David beheld the indescribable glory of the Lord, he was struck by his own utter unworthiness in comparison. *"When I consider Your heavens, the work of Your fingers, the moon and the stars, which you have ordained;*

What is man that You should take thought of him, and the son of man that You should care for him?" (v.3-4). It was clearly a "You are God, and I am not" moment. We all need more of those.

We previously discussed the effect that Paul and Silas' worship had on their perspective during their difficult imprisonment (Acts 16). That heavenly viewpoint undoubtedly influenced many of their significant decisions that followed. Now in Psalm 73, we get to read the struggles of the psalmist in his own words. *"For I was envious of the arrogant as I saw the prosperity of the wicked" (v.3)* and *"When I pondered to understand this, it was troublesome in my sight" (v.16).* So the change in his perspective is so profound in verse 17: *"Until I came into the sanctuary of God; then I perceived their end."* What a perfect picture of the power of laying it all down before God's throne! He went from *"I was senseless and ignorant; I was like a beast before You" (v.22)* to *"My flesh and my heart may fail, But God is the strength of my heart and my portion forever" (v.26).*

Being in God's presence, and therefore being reminded of who He is in all His glory, brings about a powerful transformation of our perspective on everything else in our life. The things that weigh so heavily on us when we're looking at them with our earthly mind's eye are supernaturally lifted in the light of declaring who He is. It's a healing power for the heart and mind. It's a way to peace, joy, hope, and strength not found anywhere else. And the things that we tend to hold as most valuable – that seize our greatest affections – quickly fade as the light of His glorious majesty and holiness penetrates our hearts in worship. Perspective.

2) Conviction – Conviction of sin is another inevitable transformation that results from intimate worship. **Now read Isaiah 6:1-7 and Psalm 25:1-5, 8-11.**

In lesson 4 we discussed the necessity of having *"clean hands"* and a *"pure heart"* (Ps.24:4) to enter God's presence to worship. But it only makes sense that when imperfect men encounter the holy and perfect God, we would see those broken places that still need exposure to His light in the process. It's a step that's vital to the entering of worship, as well as to the continuation of worship.

"Holy, Holy, Holy, is the LORD of hosts . . . Woe is me, for I am ruined! . . . For my eyes have seen the King, the LORD of hosts" (Isaiah 6:3,5). I love Isaiah's impassioned repentance in response to His breathtaking vision of the Lord. David had the same plea when remembering the goodness and faithfulness of his God in worship. *"To you, O LORD, I lift up my soul. . . . Lead me in Your truth and teach me, For You are the God of my salvation; For You I wait all the day. . . . For Your name's sake, O LORD, Pardon my iniquity, for it is great" (Psalm 25:1, 5, 11).* An immediate, contrite response at any prompting of the Holy Spirit will be met with not only embracing forgiveness, but with invigorated intimacy in worship.

3) Supplication – Being drawn into a time of supplication is also a transforming result that takes place during worship. **Read Psalm 19:1-14 and Psalm 86:1-12.**

As we center our focus on God in times of worship – seeing Him more clearly, declaring who He is – the result is often that God reveals our own needs in the process. As David entered prayer in a time of great distress in Psalm 86, he wisely used it as a time to focus on God and worship, to help put his need in perspective with who God is. *"You, Lord, are good, and ready to forgive, and abundant in lovingkindness to all who call upon You. Give ear, O LORD, to my prayer; And give heed to the voice of my supplications!" (v.5-6).* And as he declared the glory of God and the perfection of His law, David again responded with a personal appeal: *"Let the words of my mouth and the meditation of my heart be acceptable in Your sight, O LORD, my Rock and my Redeemer" (Psalm 19:14).* Our single focus in worship needs to be on our glorious God and not on our long list of requests. However, we need to be quick, like

David, any time the Holy Spirit prompts us to respond to the God we're exalting with a revealed need. God's Spirit longs to usher us through our time of worship.

4) Guidance – Transforming worship also makes us sensitive to the Holy Spirit's guidance. **Now read Acts 13:1-3** (noting that *"ministering to the Lord"* refers to worshiping) **and Isaiah 6:1-8** (noting that verse 8 begins with *"Then"*).

It's obvious by now that true worship involves surrender, and that includes an increased sensitivity to God's voice and leading in our lives. Warren Wiersbe said, "It's when we worship God that we discover afresh that His thoughts and ways are so far above ours that whatever we do will have to be guided and empowered by Him."[1] We should long to know God so intimately that our worship of Him puts us in that place of seeing His ways, hearing His thoughts, and longing to walk in them wherever they go. We want to hear when He says, *"Set apart . . . I have called"* (Acts 13:2) and be able to respond with *"Here am I. Send me!"* (Isaiah 6:8).

5) Desire for heaven – Gazing on the Lord during worship also increases our desire for heaven. **Read Psalm 23:1-3, 6 and Psalm 27:1-4.**

This is just a rehearsal! The link between our present lives on earth and our future in heaven is worship. Worship is central. Worship is eternal. And the more we worship in the here and now, the more we long for that non-ceasing worship service. *"One thing I have asked from the LORD, that I shall seek: That I may dwell in the house of the LORD all the days of my life, To behold the beauty of the LORD And to meditate in His temple"* (Psalm 27:4). *"Surely goodness and lovingkindness will follow me all the days of my life, And I will dwell in the house of the LORD forever"* (Psalm 23:6). It's completely unimaginable!

6) Spiritual Transformation – Basking in the amazing presence of God in worship brings about a powerful, spiritual transformation from the inside out. **Read Exodus 34:29-35 and 2 Corinthians 3:18 before continuing.**

The story of Moses coming down off of Mount Sinai with the Ten Commandments is perhaps the most dramatic worship transformation scene in the Bible. Matt Redman says that this Exodus passage "gives us insight into two things: the deep revelation of God, and the change it brings to those who experience it. The greater the revelation, the greater the transformation. Unveiled in his worship and given incredible access to the presence of God, Moses also became a changed worshipper who glowed with the glory of God."[2]

As unlikely as it is that any of us will acquire the type of radiance that Moses exhibited, the Bible tells us that we absolutely can reflect God's glory. Looking at 2 Corinthians 3:18 again, we read, *"And we, who with unveiled faces all reflect the Lord's glory, are being transformed into his likeness with ever-increasing glory, which comes from the Lord, who is the Spirit" (NIV)*. In that verse Paul reflects on Moses' experience and says that we, too, can be transformed as unveiled worshipers. In *Destined for the Throne*, Paul Billheimer concurs saying, " . . . as one worships and praises, he is continually transformed step by step, from glory to glory, into the image of the infinitely happy God."[3] I believe this change begins with an increased evidence of the fruit of the Spirit in our lives (Galatians 5:22). I like the way John Wimber explains the transformation: "As we interact with God, we will find ourselves more and more satisfied in Him, and less and less satisfied with the things that have attracted or enticed us."[4] This is a transformation that goes way beyond just one's perspective. This is life-altering transformation. It's a change that is recognizable from the outside but surely begins with a transformation in the inner man. How would it change your life if you were more and more satisfied in God and were less and less satisfied with the things that normally entice you? Oh, pray that would be your heart's desire!

Of course, it shouldn't be surprising that the Bible shows us how reflection results for those who worship idols as well: *"Those who make them will become like them, everyone who trusts in them"* (Psalm 115:8). We see this happening all throughout our culture today.

Again, these transformations we just looked at are results of the inner work of the Spirit of God in our lives when we bow in worship. We also find evidence of how these inner workings can result in more outward effects.

7) Encouragement – Worship amongst believers inspires encouragement. **Now read Psalm 34:1-3 and Psalm 69:30-32.**

When we worship together, our words, proclaiming and adoring who God is, encourage and stimulate others in their faith and walk with Him. *"My soul will make its boast in the LORD; The humble will hear it and rejoice. O magnify the LORD with me, And let us exalt His name together"* (Psalm 34:2-3). *"I will praise the name of God with song and magnify Him with thanksgiving . . . The humble have seen it and are glad; You who seek God, let your heart revive"* (Psalm 69:30, 32). True worship encourages others in their relationships with God and reproduces more worship! It's vitally important to a healthy, impactful church to get worship right!

8) Unity – Related to encouragement, transforming worship brings about unity. **Reread Psalm 34:1-3 and then Acts 2:46-47.**

We've already looked at these verses, but they show the additional display of God's power in encouraging unity in the lives of believers who worship together. It's the most powerful thing that the body of Christ can share! *"Day by day continuing with one mind in the temple, and breaking bread from house to house, they were taking their meals **together** with gladness and sincerity of heart, praising God and having favor with all the people"* (Acts 2:46-47a). *"My soul will make* *its boast in the LORD; The humble will hear it and rejoice. O magnify the LORD with me, And let us exalt His name **together**" (Psalm 34:2-3).* The revelation of God in authentic worship has the power to bring unity to those lifting His name together.

9) Evangelism – Another powerful outward effect of worship is evangelism. **Read Psalm 40:3 and Acts 16:25-34.**

I must admit that even after spending over 20 years in both evangelistic and worship music ministry, I'd always tended to err on the *safe* side of evangelizing when it came to music – which definitely didn't include worship. I think Satan wants us to think that worshiping our Savior is so foreign to the lost that it would always push them further away from Him. But these passages prove that line of thinking false. We see evidence of that in the powerful story of Paul and Silas (Acts 16). There's obviously something supernatural that happens when we lift the name of our God for all to see. *"He put a new song in my mouth, a song of praise to our God; Many will see and fear and will trust in the LORD" (Psalm 40:3).* It's unexplainable. It's convicting!

10) Help in battle – One of the most extraordinary examples of God's display of power in response to worship is that of His movement in times of battle. **Read 2 Chronicles 20:1-24 and Daniel 3:10-30.** (Remember Paul and Silas from Acts 16 again, as well.)

Jehoshaphat wisely led his people to seek and worship God as his first response to the news of a great army advancing toward them to attack. God knows that Satan fears the worship of God most of all. So when Judah went out before the army and proclaimed, *"Give thanks to the Lord, for His lovingkindness is everlasting" (v21)*, there couldn't have been a more devastating assault on the approaching enemy! The Daniel passage also shows how God protected men who refused to worship other gods in the face of life-threatening danger. Shadrach, Meshach, and Abednego did this knowing full well that God could choose to *not* save them. But He *did* save them. And not only that, the kingdom, and eventually the world, heard of God's miraculous deliverance of His worshipers, as a result of their heathen king responding with a decree against the very idolatry that was the reason for his attempt on their lives to begin with. I believe *this* truly was God's greater goal – the powerful glory brought to His name as a result!

That's a short, and obviously incomplete, look at what God does in the lives of His children in response to their faithful, diligent worship. It's also another incredible picture of who He is – of His incredible love for us and His amazing grace towards us. It's easy to put Biblical characters in a different category from ourselves. We tend to see them as more spiritually mature, more knowledgeable, and even more lovable to God. But they needed to confess their sins just like us. They struggled with self-centeredness, distractions, apathy – all of the same things that threaten to take us away from worshiping God. Yet they continued to strive towards the goal to become the worshipers that He made them to be. And as a result, He blessed them with greater revelations of Himself – just like He longs to do for us. Chances are pretty good that we may never see prison chains fall off or enemy armies fall over dead. But we'll surely see His transforming power working in our hearts, minds, and lives, if we just keep pursuing His grand purpose for us – that of becoming worshipers of the Almighty God. Maybe that's a greater work! So let's keep striving!

Pause: to reflect and pray

As I look over these different expressions of God's power displayed in worship, what do they tell me about God?

Have I ever experienced God in any of these ways as a result of fervent worship? How?

Which ones jump out as areas that I would like to see personally realized in my life? Why?

How does this look at God's response to worship affect my view of worship in the church?

Ask God to continue to give you a passion to become the worshiper He made you to be. Ask Him to help you to see Him more clearly so you can worship Him more deeply. Ask Him to reveal His power to you in new ways.

Now spend some time worshiping before Him.

PLACE

I love You, O LORD, my strength.
The LORD is my rock and my fortress and my deliverer,
My God, my rock in whom I take refuge;
My shield and the horn of my salvation, my stronghold.
I call upon the LORD, who is worthy to be praised,
and I am saved from my enemies.
The LORD lives, and blessed be my rock;
and exalted be the God of my salvation.

Psalm 18: 1-3, 46

Lesson Eight

The PLACE for Worship

There's not a PLACE life can take us where it's not appropriate, even necessary, to worship God.

For regardless of what that place looks like or feels like, the God we worship hasn't changed. Whatever the place, God is saying to us, as in Psalm 46:10, "Cease striving! Stop! Be still! And know that I am God! The result will be a heart that longs to worship me" (my paraphrase).

When my daughters were younger and I wanted to tell them something that I really needed for them to hear, I would frequently begin by saying, "Look at me." After I had eye contact with them, I would say what I needed to say. If one of them was in a more active, distracted mode, and didn't hear or respond to my initial request, then I would sometimes place my hand on her cheek to gently direct her face towards mine to get her attention. I picture God doing that same thing with me. Sometimes He says, "Look at Me," and I hear and obey. Other times I am extremely distracted, and He needs to gently put His hand on my cheek and turn my face toward His to get my attention. If I don't fight the attempt, then the result is an intimate moment with Him, resulting in a desire to worship the God who has wooed me into His presence.

Whether life is calm or hectic, joyful or painful, we need constant reminders of who God is in the midst of that place. Sometimes it feels like the *"mountains have slipped into the heart of the sea"* *(Psalm 46:2)*, but God is *still* God. He's still good, faithful, merciful, and loving. Sometimes everything seems to be going my way, and God is *still* God. He's still my light, my hope, my forgiver, and my wisdom. God is fully God – all that He says He is – at all times. No amount of turmoil, or confusion, or victory changes that truth. That's reason enough to worship Him!

There are multitudes of Biblical examples of worshiping God in various places of life. I've placed them in three categories – places of difficulty, blessing, and revelation. Let's look at each one.

1) Places of difficulty – Did you know that 70 percent of the Psalms are laments, written from places of crying out to God? Yet they never challenge who God is or His worth.[11] Instead, they reveal Him as the source of hope. They claim His goodness, greatness, and faithfulness. If we begin with one of David's psalms that we discussed briefly in Lesson 4, we'll learn quite a bit.

Read Psalm 63 from your own Bible.

David wrote Psalm 63 when he was in the wilderness of Judah, probably after he fled Jerusalem at the time of Absalom's rebellion (2 Samuel 15). Obviously, the place David is in at this point in his life isn't all that great. God was protecting him, but He hadn't changed the situation yet. David knows his need to seek God, and seeks Him *"earnestly"* *(v.1)*. He does this by entering the *"sanctuary"* *(v.2)*, or place of worship, *"to see [His] power and [His] glory"* *(v.2)*. Why? Because he already knows by experience that God's *"lovingkindness is better than life"* *(v.3)*, and he knows his need to verbalize it once more. After all, his *"life"* was on the line (v.9)! So this was David's expression of faith and the beginning of worship to the God that he knew intimately. As David continues to lift up who God is, he finds *"satisfaction" (v.5)* for his soul. He then continues to *"remember" (v.6)* God's faithfulness and strength in the past, leading to an increase in his faith and reliance on God for his current situation.

We begin to feel defeat *"in the dry and weary land where there is no water" (v.1),* when we fail to recognize that we *"thirst"* and *"yearn" (v.1)* for God. We don't strive to *"see" (v.2)* Him there, and therefore, we fail to drink to quench the thirst. We don't *"remember" (v.6)* who He is and then fail to worship Him. The end result is that we fail to find the satisfaction (v.5), increased faith, strength, and even *"joy" (v.7)* that He makes available to us.

David wasn't in denial about his situation. He was living in the midst of the reality of *who God was for him* in that situation. That reality was only found because David chose to worship. Just like the people of Judah and Paul and Silas later on, David found the barrier-breaking power of worship when he came face to face with the God who sees – the God who avenges, the God who overcomes, my Hiding Place, my Mighty Rock – in a very difficult place. In *that* place, David found strength, hope, and healing.

Now read the following verses from your own Bible, and find the difficult place that led to worship there. (It helps to look for words such as "because" and "for," as well as worshipful actions, such as bowing, etc.)

Example: Matthew 8: 2-3 - the leper needed healing; he bowed down before Jesus.

2 Samuel 12:9, 13-17, 19-20

Job 1:13-22

Psalm 71:1-20

Matthew 9:18

Hebrews 11:21

Warren Wiersbe says, "*It is our regular worship that prepares us for the crisis experiences of life.* What life does to us depends on what life finds in us."[2] May the difficult places of life find in *us* hearts that comprehend the power of God's presence and glory in worship and therefore choose to bow before Him once again.

2) Places of blessing – Worshiping God in a place of blessing is so much easier. Right? Not necessarily! It's very easy for us to become accustomed to feeling blessed, so much so that we forget where the blessings come from. This is especially true when you're from a blessed family or blessed country. We tend to take the simple things for granted, subconsciously believing we deserve them or are responsible ourselves for all the good things around us. And it's easy to become self-absorbed, distracted, or just plain apathetic. That's why, as we've discussed in previous lessons, it's important that our first pursuit be that of knowing and loving God, *out of which* will grow a desire to worship Him as a way of life. Let's look at some people who chose to exalt God in their place of blessing. Some are simple examples, and some are amazing ones.

Read Luke 17: 12-19.

Here we have a good example of one who chose to stop to glorify Jesus, and others who chose not to. I can't personally imagine a blessing any greater than that of being healed by something as horrible as leprosy. It's even harder to imagine that out of ten men who saw Jesus face to face and knew that He Himself had healed them, only one stopped to give glory to his Healer. Yet, I'd hate to read a list of blessings, big or small, for which I've failed to thank and glorify God, especially since we see here that Jesus didn't just recognize the one that returned, but grieved the nine that didn't.

Now read the following verses, and identify the place of blessing that led to worship there.

Exodus 14:26 - 15:2

Psalm 21:1-6, 13

Psalm 34:1-4

Luke 1:39-50

1 Timothy 1:12-17

We need to *choose* to be the worshipers that God intended. We need to recognize and give glory to the God who so graciously and generously gives us the blessings in our lives. What pleasure we bring to our Heavenly Father when we say, *"My soul will make its boast in the Lord!" (Psalm 34:2).*

3) Places of revelation – God has committed Himself to revealing to us the truths about who He is and how He works. Jeremiah 29:13 says, " . . . *you will seek Me and find Me, when you search for Me with all your heart."* The more intimately we know Him, the quicker we'll recognize His truths, His hand, and His movements when they come our way. God also chooses at times to use events to open the eyes of the spiritually blind to finally see who He is. After all, He longs for everyone to be saved! Let's look at some people who bowed and worshiped in response to His revelation in their lives.

Read Daniel 3:24-29.

Here's that familiar story again of Shadrach, Meshach, and Abednego. I love King Nebuchadnezzar's response to the fiery furnace incident. While it's true that it was hard to deny what had just happened, Nebuchadnezzar didn't hesitate. He said, *"Blessed be the God of Shadrach, Meshach, and Abednego" (v.28)*! While this was quite the revealing moment, I think that if we really looked, we too, would see God's hand in more places than we could imagine.

There are also God's revelations of Himself around us in nature that should prompt our hearts to bow in worship. *"And one called out to another and said, 'Holy, Holy, Holy, is the LORD of hosts, the whole earth is full of His glory'" (Isaiah 6:3)*. The literal translation is "the fullness of the whole earth is His glory." Do we take time to view God's revelation of Himself around us for the amazing thing it is, and respond to Him in worship?

Now read the following verses, and describe the revelations that led to worship there.

Exodus 34:1-8

Psalm 66:1-6, 16-20

Matthew 5:16

John 9:13-15, 32-38

Romans 11: 33-36

1 Peter 1: 6-7

The greater the vision of our spiritual eyes, the greater our response in worship will be – for we'll be constantly filled with awe at who He is and what He does. *"Say to God, 'How awesome are Your works! Because of the greatness of Your power Your enemies will give feigned obedience to You. All the earth will worship You'" (Psalm 66:3-4a)*. The revelation of God is that powerful! We should be quick at each glorious display to say, *"Lord, I believe"* *(John 9:8)*, *"to Him be the glory forever"* *(Romans 11: 36)*, and offer Him our worship!

We could go on and on. But I think these verses are more than adequate to show that, again, there's not a place life can take us where it's not appropriate, even necessary, to worship God. A.W. Tozer said, "The heart that knows God can find God anywhere. A person filled with the Spirit of God, a person who has met God in a living encounter can know the joy of worshiping Him, whether in the silences of life or in the storms of life."[3] And I don't know if you've noticed, but there are more Biblical examples of people worshiping God privately than there are of them worshiping as a body of believers. He requires both. But do we take the time and opportunity for both? The fact that it pleases God is enough. But the work that He does in our hearts and minds, as a result (see Lesson 7), is enormous. We desperately need to learn to *"be still"* and *"know that He is God"* *(Psalm 46:10)* – and fall on our knees in response to what we see. In all places. At all times. Because God is God.

Pause: to reflect and pray

Of the three different places of worship – difficulty, blessing, and revelation – which one comes the most easily to me, and which the most difficult? Why?

Which situation/verse in each category can I relate to most easily? How?

Did I choose to worship or even acknowledge God at those times? Why or why not?

Do I struggle with even wanting to worship God in certain situations? Explain.

Pray an honest prayer, expressing your heart to God in this area. Ask Him to help you remember who He is in the midst of life's difficulties, blessings, and revelations of truth. Ask Him to help you see His hand at work around you and in you. Worship Him for His faithfulness, goodness, and lovingkindness in answering your prayer.

POSTURE

Praise the LORD!
Sing to the LORD a new song,
And His praise in the congregation of the godly ones.
Let them praise His name with dancing;
Let them sing praises to Him with timbrel and lyre.
For the LORD takes pleasure in His people;

Psalm 149:1, 3-4a

Behold, bless the LORD, all servants of the LORD,
Who serve by night in the house of the LORD!
Lift up your hands to the sanctuary and bless the LORD.

Psalm 134:1-2

Lesson Nine

Our POSTURE in Worship

The Bible calls worshipers to not only have bowed hearts and minds, but to have a POSTURE that is yielded to the Holy Spirit and that engages our entire being before God.

The previous lessons have taken us into the very necessary and primary internal elements of worship. Now let's look at topics involving our outer expressions of worship. Obviously, some of these tend to be the more controversial matters, not only from church to church, but from person to person, as well. Unfortunately, often our opinions are based more on personal taste and just what we grew up doing, rather than on what the Bible offers on the subject. So we need to explore further.

Looking back at the first lesson, we see that the Hebrew and Greek literal meanings for the words translated *worship* or *praise* throughout the Bible are very active words. A few we looked at were:

> *halal* – to worship exuberantly or in an unbridled manner
> *shachah* – to bow down before
> *yadah* – to extend the hand to God
> *proskuneo* – to bow and kiss

Studying worship throughout the Bible, I don't think it takes long to realize that there is absolutely nothing passive about the act of worship. Nothing. But you wouldn't know that to observe many "worship" services in Christian churches today. What would the typical non-Christian observer quickly assume was our attitude toward our God, if he or she scrutinized the average church service? Would they walk away with any desire to know *that* God, based on the expressions of the Christians they saw there?

Let's unpack a few topics involved in our posture before God in worship, see what the Bible has to say, and find some foundational truths to stand on.

1) Lifting hands – *"Because Your lovingkindness is better than life, My lips will praise You. So I will praise You. So I will bless You as long as I live; I will **lift up my hands** in Your name" (Psalm 63:3-4).*

*"Hear the voice of my supplications when I cry to You for help, When I **lift up my hands** toward Your holy sanctuary" (Psalm 28:2).*

*"Behold, bless the LORD, all servants of the LORD, Who serve by night in the house of the LORD! **Lift up your hands** to the sanctuary and bless the LORD" (Psalm 134:1-2).*

*"May my prayer be counted as incense before You; The **lifting up of my hands** as the evening offering" (Psalm 141:2)*

*"I **stretch out my hands** to You; My soul longs for You, as a parched land" (Psalm 142:6).*

I recently heard Israel Houghton say, "Both hands raised is the international sign for surrender. Regardless of what language you speak, if you see somebody with both hands up, then they're saying, 'I give up. You're bigger. You win.' We decrease and He increases in that moment."[12] I like that. When we lift our hands to God, we're acknowledging a heart of surrender – acknowledging His greatness in relation to us. Our culture doesn't seem too comfortable with lifting our hands to God in public though. I think that part of that has to do with the fact that it is a very intimate, personal response toward God. I spent many years not getting my hands above my shoulders during public worship. But I discovered that as I allowed myself to enjoy the lifting of my hands in times of private worship, I wanted to enjoy it publicly, as well. I think that was because, for me personally, my hands are very connected with my mind. If my hands are uninvolved, then my mind tends to be less involved. But I've heard people whom I respect tremendously say that they're raising their hands big time on the inside, though it may not be noticeable on the outside. And I believe them. I would just encourage you to not write it off, never try it, or even discourage it, for it could be the hidden secret to increasing the tunnel vision of your own worship. As I've grown in my ability to block out things and people around me in public worship (okay, except for crying babies), then I really find that the lifting of my hands feels like a private expression even there. I frequently reach out to touch or embrace those I love, and God is at the top of that list.

2) Bowing/Kneeling – After the Lord passed in front of Moses, proclaiming who He was, *"Moses made haste to **bow low toward the earth** and worship"* *(Exodus 34:8).*

*"All the sons of Israel, seeing the fire come down and the glory of the LORD upon the house, **bowed down on the pavement with their faces to the ground**, and they worshiped and gave praise to the LORD, saying, 'Truly He is good, truly His lovingkindness is everlasting'"* *(2 Chronicles 7:3).*

*"Then Ezra blessed the LORD the great God. And all the people answered, "Amen, Amen!" while lifting up their hands; then they **bowed low** and worshiped the LORD **with their faces to the ground**"* *(Nehemiah 8:6).*

*"Because He is your Lord, **bow down** to Him"* *(Psalm 45:11b).*

*"Come let us worship and **bow down**, Let us **kneel** before the LORD our Maker" (Psalm 95:6).*

*"I will **bow down** toward Your holy temple and give thanks to Your name for Your lovingkindness and Your truth" (Psalm 138:2).*

*"Exalt the LORD our God and worship **at His footstool**: Holy is He" (Psalm 99:5).*

*"For it is written, 'As I live, says the Lord, **every knee shall bow** to Me, And every tongue shall give praise to God'" (Romans 14:11).*

Again, here's another action that we sing about all the time, but rarely do, unlike some other cultures. Yet the Bible is full of examples of people who encounter God and then fall to their knees in response to His overwhelming glory. Matt Redman says, "When we really pay attention to God's worth, our worship times will start to look even more like the heavenly throne room. The angels sing, as do we. The living creatures speak out their praise, and we join them. But the 24 elders bow down on their faces. Oh, that we would see what they see and do as they do, a little more often! **To bow is the ultimate physical sign of reverence**" (emphasis mine).[2]

Lazarus' sister, Mary, bowed to anoint Jesus' feet with expensive perfume, and He defended her actions to her critics (John 12:1-8). Bowing is physically acting out the position of our bowed hearts before God. I believe that God wants us to learn what it means to literally *proskuneo*, or "bow and kiss" Him. And again, I personally know that the position of my body greatly affects the direction of my mind. I'm obviously not saying you have to do this in church on Sunday (though your pastor or worship leader may invite that at times), but find a place where you can express the depth of that kind of reverence and affection. My guess is that you'll return often.

3) Clapping – *"O **clap** your hands, all peoples; Shout to God with the voice of joy"* *(Psalm 47:1).*

*"Let the rivers **clap** their hands, let the mountains sing together for joy before the LORD"* *(Psalm 98:8-9a).*

Even God's creation claps its hands in joy to the Lord! We do a little better in this area, though sometimes half-heartedly. We seem to have no problem clapping and cheering for our favorite sports team (I include myself in that!), yet the God of the universe seems to get the remnants of our joyful expressions. I'm sure He longs to see us express the joy that His salvation, blessings, and very presence have brought into our lives. I'm not talking about clapping for performers in a worship service. In true worship, our focus should only be on Him who is truly deserving of our praise. Don't fear expressing yourself in new ways in your worship. Fear becoming detached, lifeless, or apathetic.

4) Dancing – *"Let them praise His name with **dancing**; Let them sing praises to Him with timbrel and lyre. For the LORD takes pleasure in His people"* *(Psalm 149:3-4a).*

*"Praise him with timbrel and **dancing**. Let everything that has breath praise the LORD"* *(Psalm 150:4a, 6).*

*"And so it was, that when the bearers of the ark of the LORD had gone six paces, he sacrificed an ox and a fatling. And David was **dancing** before the LORD with all his might"* *(2 Samuel 6:13-14).*

In case you weren't uncomfortable enough with the ideas of lifting your hands, bowing, and clapping, I thought I'd take it to the next level! I think the point of each of these is that when we've been invaded by the knowledge and love of God, then the natural resulting worship may take on forms that are quite a bit more demonstrative than when we were casual, distant viewers of God.

For God is not a casual God! And David's dancing was a beautiful act of worship to Him. (If you read a little further in 2 Samuel, not everyone thought so!) Of course, this will look different for different people. We're individuals who don't express ourselves alike in our earthly relationships, and this is no different. But the goal is to allow God to move in and through us, so that our worship brings Him the most glory and allows us to experience His presence most deeply.

Now my favorite: *"The LORD your God is in your midst, a victorious warrior. He will exult over you with joy, He will be quiet in His love, He will rejoice over you with shouts of joy"* (Zephaniah 3:17). Remember, the Hebrew word for *"rejoice"* in this verse literally means "to spin around with intense motion" or "to dance or leap for joy." As mentioned in Lesson 4, God's love for us is so profound that He exuberantly dances for joy over us! I know that I'm not worthy of His dance apart from the work of Jesus on my behalf. But He's more than worthy of whatever exuberance I can muster in response to all He is and has done for me. So why not dance!

Although these first four points are aimed at encouraging those who may be more inhibited in expressing worship in a physical manner, I want to address those who read them and automatically think, *not my problem!* Be careful not to enter a time of worship with a focus other than that of our holy God. It's especially easy for some to enter a worship service at church thinking, *love the music, love the beat, love the people,* and express exuberance for the wrong reasons. If that's you, then there may even be a need to dial it back so you can refocus on God. These actions are encouraged biblically as a means to enhance your expression of worship, not to be a distraction from it.

To have a posture that's yielded and engaged before God in worship, it's import to consider how the posture of our *minds* and *attitudes* affects different aspects of our worship. This is especially true in our times of corporate worship with other believers. To say that the change in worship styles in churches over the past few decades has been an adjustment for some people is putting it mildly. And it's important that we don't allow small issues to suddenly distract us or cause us to become critical of what's going on, instead of continuing in an attitude of worship. I'm sure there are many other issues I could cover, but these next two are common topics that have come up in many of my conversations that I believe have biblical precedent.

5) Repeating words – Have you ever heard anyone who is new to contemporary worship music complain about repeating words that they've already sung again and again? I didn't know what a big issue this was to some until recently, even hearing of a code language used between groups of people in church to basically express "there they go again, repeating a phrase." I tend to think that if their hearts and minds were actually focused on worshiping – on truly expressing the words they were lifting to God – that they wouldn't mind so much. After all, don't young lovers enjoy saying and hearing "I love you" over and over? This is no different. Jesus is our bridegroom! Plus, I know for myself, sometimes it takes repeating a truth again and again before it deeply connects with my heart and mind. Let's see if we can find some Biblical support for this.

The most obvious example is Psalm 136: *"Give thanks to the LORD, for He is good, **For His lovingkindness is everlasting**. Give thanks to the God of gods, **For His lovingkindness is everlasting**. Give thanks to the Lord of lords, **For His lovingkindness is everlasting**. To Him who alone does great wonders, **For His lovingkindness is everlasting**. To Him who made the heavens with skill, **For His lovingkindness is everlasting**. To Him who spread out the earth above the waters, **For His lovingkindness is everlasting**."* (This goes on and on for 26 verses!)

I remember reading this when I was younger and thinking, *Yikes! What were they thinking? Let's get on with it.* But the psalmist obviously wanted to get across the point that God really did all of these things – and still does *everything* – out of His unending love for us. And then in Psalm 115, the psalmist wanted to make sure we really understood that we need to trust the Lord and why.

*"O Israel, trust in the LORD; **He is their help and their shield**. O house of Aaron, trust in the LORD; **He is their help and their shield**. You who fear the LORD, trust in the LORD; **He is their help and their shield**" (Psalm 115:9-11).*

Sometimes repetition just helps us get the point. If I'm focused on sincerely communicating the truths of the words I'm singing to my God, then I don't care how many times I sing it, and He definitely never tires of hearing it. Often those moments in songs that cover less content provide much needed space for our minds to be still and mediate on a penetrating Biblical truth. Or they allow us to lean in more closely to the revealed glory of God, and allow *Him* to press in more intimately on us with an even greater wonder of who He is.

Remember when Jesus asked Peter three times in John 21:15-17, *"Do you love Me?"* I think Peter got a little irritated at the repeated question, but by the last time, His answer, though similar, changed in its focus. I think Jesus got His point across.

The one repetition that we're familiar with and accept so freely is this: *Holy, Holy, Holy!* In Isaiah's vision, he was describing the worship of the seraphim in Isaiah 6:3. *"And one called out to another and said, 'Holy, Holy, Holy, is the LORD of hosts, The whole earth is full of His glory.'"* And this description of God is repeated in Revelation 4:8. *". . . day and night they do not cease to say, 'Holy, holy, holy, is the Lord God Almighty, who was and who is and who is to come!'"* We're comfortable repeating the word holy, because of the most loved hymn. But why is it repeated in these Bible verses to begin with? I think it's because God isn't just holy. He is truly HOLY, HOLY, HOLY! We're commanded in several places (Leviticus 11:44 and 1 Peter 1:16, among others), *"You shall be holy, for I am holy."* We're called to be holy. But HE is HOLY, HOLY, HOLY! I think that if we could add a quite a few more holies, it would still describe our God perfectly, and our human minds would still not grasp the depths this important truth. But this repetition is oh so necessary, and oh so significant, when describing our holy God.

I'm obviously not saying everything has to be repeated x-number of times. But when you're in that situation, instead of letting your mind wander into why-are-we-doing-this mode, make each repetition a new aim to understand, connect, and communicate the words in a deeper way as you express them to God. Repetition may then become your friend.

6) Singing new songs – One Sunday I attended a different church from my own to join my husband, John, who was playing the keyboards there that day. It was a church that had a history of using traditional music but was trying to work in some newer choruses. I ended up sitting next to a much older, gray-haired gentleman, and though we hadn't spoken to each other beyond the friendly greeting, we ended up sharing a hymnal during a couple of songs. At the end of the service he turned and looked at me, and said, completely out of nowhere, "Do you know what two-thirds of the word *contemporary* is? (Pause.) Temporary!" I was completely stunned, since we hadn't spoken before this. And in my bewildered state, I just replied, "Oh, that's interesting," and then we parted. As far as I know, he couldn't tell that I was married to the different keyboardist who obviously enjoyed playing the "contemporary" stuff. Maybe I sounded like I enjoyed singing the newer songs more than he liked. I don't know. I just knew that it made no sense, since all songs are "contemporary" at the time of their writing and are obviously not all "temporary." But beyond that, I knew that he missed out on a tremendous blessing by not having opened his heart and mind to the words that the worship leader was guiding us in. The Bible just happens to have something to say on this topic, too.

*"He put **a new song** in my mouth, a song of praise to our God; Many will see and fear and will trust in the LORD" (Psalm 40:3).*

*"Sing to Him **a new song**; Play skillfully with a shout of joy" (Psalm 33:3).*

*"O sing to the LORD **a new song**, For He has done wonderful things, His right hand and His holy arm have gained the victory for Him" (Psalm 98:1).*

*"Praise the LORD! Sing to the LORD **a new song**, And His praise in the congregation of the godly ones" (Psalm 149:1).*

*"When He had taken the book, the four living creatures and the twenty-four elders fell down before the Lamb, each one holding a harp and golden bowls full of incense, which are the prayers of the saints. And they sang a **new song**, saying, 'Worthy are You to take the book and to break its seals; for You were slain, and purchased for God with Your blood men from every tribe and tongue and people and nation'" (Revelation 5:8-9).*

According to Revelation 5:8-9, we can expect to hear and sing new songs at the ultimate worship service for all time! Now is not the time to get so comfortable with the old and current that we end up just mouthing words that we've sung for years. (I've been guilty of that.) As our knowledge and our relationship with God grow, so should the depths of our worship expression, with new words, new insights, new melodies, and new expressions of adoration. Sure, we'll have our favorites, but we need to bring Him new gifts, as well. I think God would surely delight at our own attempts at writing poems, songs, or letters of exaltation and adoration to Him. After all, Jesus is our Song (Psalm 118:14; Isaiah 12:2). And as we respond in worship to each new revelation or new blessing of grace, we sing His song! In Psalm 40:3, after being delivered out of *"the pit of destruction,"* God then *"put a new song"* in David's mouth, *"a song of praise to our God."* So don't be afraid to pour out your heart before Him in new ways. And delight in the songs He gives to others. He may just want them to be *your* new song, too.

The goal of studying these points is not to make everyone act the same. But it's to encourage you to pour *all of who God created you to be* into your worship of Him, *and* to respect others who do so, as well. This I know: Satan utterly despises our worship of God and will do anything in his power to stop it. His tactics are subtle and effective. So we need to be very careful to guard our worshiping hearts – to bathe them in prayer. If the enemy can distract us – get us to nitpick and criticize others in the body of Christ, judging their worship style or their music (he who has ears, let him hear), instead of engaging in worship ourselves – then he's won a huge battle. And we've lost. And we walk away empty and void of what God wants to do in our hearts as His worshipers, instead of full of the glory of God.

Now we've all seen or heard of churches that seem over the top on some of these topics and appear to value emotionalism over genuineness and show over substance. That is neither our goal nor a reason to be swayed from really hearing what the Bible teaches. Throwing the baby out with the bathwater, like the church has tended to do, isn't the solution. But studying His Word and individually seeking Him in prayer as to how we should each individually respond is the best course.

God undoubtedly loves the unique way He created each one of us. And as Christians, we know that as truly different as we are from one another (and think about that from a global perspective!), we all worship the *very same God* – through the drawing and direction of the *very same Spirit*. I like how A.W. Tozer put it: "The Holy Spirit does not operate by anyone's preconceived idea or formula. But this I know: when the Holy Spirit of God comes among us with His anointing, we become a worshiping people. This may be hard to admit, but when we are truly worshiping and adoring the God of all grace and of all love and of all mercy and of all truth, we may not be quiet enough to please everyone[3] . . . [yet] even the faintest whisper will be worship.[4]"

Pause: to reflect and pray

How would I describe my current posture during my times of worship: intimate, passionate, yielded, engaged, cautious, detached, lifeless, stagnant, etc.? (Note: This isn't a question just about your internal posture towards God but about how you allow yourself to express it in worship.)

Am I guilty of judging how others in the body of Christ worship? What issues do I struggle with that take me to a critical place?

Has my view of any of these final six points changed after reading these scriptures? How?

Am I willing to try something that I have never tried before, even in private worship? Explain.

Invite the Holy Spirit to teach you how to grow to have a completely yielded, engaged posture as you come before His throne in worship.

PASSIONATE PURSUIT

... God highly exalted Him,
and bestowed on Him
the name which is above every name,
so that at the name of Jesus
EVERY KNEE WILL BOW,
of those who are in heaven and on earth
and under the earth,
and that every tongue will confess that
Jesus Christ is Lord,
to the glory of God the Father.

Philippians 2:9-11

Praise the LORD!
Praise, O servants of the LORD.
Praise the name of the LORD.
Blessed be the name of the LORD
from this time forth and forever.
From the rising of the sun to its setting,
the name of the LORD is to be praised.

Psalm 113:1-3

Lesson Ten

The PASSIONATE PURSUIT of Worship

We are called to live a life that is wholly and continually engaged in the **PASSIONATE PURSUIT** to be God-worshipers.

I began this study by inviting you on the most important journey that you would ever take – to explore God's call to us to be His worshipers. And the journey doesn't stop with the end of this book, because we've barely gotten out of the parking lot. In fact, this journey will last for all of eternity! Every day is another opportunity to grow in our knowledge and love of God and in the intimate depths as His worshipers. We've waded through many Bible passages and talked about how they should influence our lives. And how we end this study, without ending the journey, is by taking the advice of the writer of Hebrews 2:1: *"For this reason* [the proven superiority of Christ from chapter 1] *we must pay much closer attention to what we have heard, so that we do not drift away from it."* We'll drift away from God's call to us to be passionate worshipers if we treat it, or His Word, casually. That's treating God Himself casually. The psalmist wisely prayed, *"Establish Your word to Your servant, as that which produces reverence for you" (Psalm 119:38).* We need to constantly nurture the soil of our hearts with regular time in His Word, time in His presence, and time worshiping the God who continues to reveal Himself to us. (Can I remind myself of that too many times?) Then His truth will grow deeper roots into our souls, and we'll be much more able to endure the constant noise and distractions, both great and small, that this world constantly throws our way and that threaten our growing devotion to God.

And those distractions might be *good* things – even ministry-related things. Anytime we place anything, good or not, in a higher position of priority above worshiping Jesus Christ, we make *it* the god, robbing Him of the glory that He alone deserves. The result is that we then rob ourselves of the rich, growing relationship with God that we were created to have. Steven Furtick says, "The King comes first! The tragedy of so many lives is that in an effort to avoid missing out on what we think matters, we end up missing out on the only thing that really matters. When we make excuses, we reflect two beliefs: #1, we don't really believe Jesus is worthy, or #2, we don't really believe this thing, [worship], is urgent. And I promise you, He is worthy, and this thing is urgent."[1]

Jesus took distractions from worship seriously. We know this from reading Matthew 21:12-13. *"Jesus entered the temple area and drove out all who were buying and selling there. He overturned the tables of the money-changers and the benches of those selling doves. 'It is written,' he said to them, 'My house will be called a house of prayer, but you are making it a den of robbers.'"* What were they robbing? They were robbing the Gentiles of their dedicated place of worship and prayer in the outer courts of the temple. He had made it clear that this was an unacceptable practice three years prior (John 2:14-16), but their businesses, even under the guise of being religious, were inhibiting worship. *Their* priority was the monetary gain of worldly business. *Jesus'* priority was the soulful gain of anyone who would choose to come and worship the Father there. While we don't sell doves and exchange currency in churches these days, we do often have things in our lives and churches that inhibit ourselves, and others around us, from worshiping the Lord. We have tables, so to speak, that desperately need to be turned over. We need to get rid of anything that weighs us down, distracts us, clutters our minds, or holds us back in any way. We need to remember and diligently fulfill the prerequisites for being true worshipers of the Most High God, such as *"clean hands and a pure heart"* from Psalm 24:3-5 (see Lesson 4), instead of believing that going through the religious motions is enough. This isn't because God wants to add to our "to do" list but because He is wholly deserving and worthy of all of our strivings to have a worshiper's devoted heart. Be bold! Flip the tables in your life that are preventing true worship!

The bar is set quite high when it comes to removing distractions to worship. If anyone could've qualified for a "grace pass" for caving to a distraction, it would've been Shadrach, Meshach, and Abednego. Looking again at Daniel 3:1-30, not only did the now-famous three not cave to the king's command to bow to his idol, but they responded with absolutely no hesitation or fear. How could they do that? They knew their God! They knew that the God they loved had come through for them previously in answering their prayers with Daniel (2:17-49), in giving Daniel the interpretation to King Nebuchadnezzar's dream, thus sparing all of their lives. And now this horrific king was at it again. *"Nebuchadnezzar . . . said to them, 'Is it true, Shadrach, Meshach and Abednego, that you do not serve my gods or worship the golden image that I have set up? . . . if you do not worship [it], you will immediately be cast into the midst of a furnace of blazing fire; and what god is there who can deliver you out of my hands?' Shadrach, Meshach and Abednego replied to the king, 'O Nebuchadnezzar, we do not need to give you an answer concerning this matter. If it be so,* **our God whom we serve is able to deliver us** *from the furnace of blazing fire; and He will deliver us out of your hand, O king.* **But even if He does not,** *let it be known to you, O king, that* **we are not going to serve your gods or worship the golden image that you have set up'"** *(Daniel 3:14-18,* emphasis mine). Of course, we all know how this dramatic story ends. An infuriated Nebuchadnezzar heats the furnace seven-times hotter than usual, and ties up and tosses in the three friends (with the heat killing the men who throw them in). Then God not only saves Shadrach, Meshach, and Abednego, but they are joined by a fourth man *"with the appearance like a son of the gods"(v.25),* and all were completely untouched and unharmed by the flames. Nebuchadnezzar responds by decreeing that no one speak against the Most High God of these men!

We cannot read any of these stories and not know beyond any doubt how passionately God feels about His call to us to be His faithful, exclusive worshipers. No one can make you or me take the necessary steps to turn over the worship-robbing tables in our lives. Nor can anyone make us refuse to bow to the demands around us that are screaming to be first on our worship priority list. Starting each day with a heart and mind set on seeking, knowing, loving, and worshiping God is essential. And filling our minds with truths from the Bible, *"the sword of the Spirit" (Ephesians 6:17),* is a necessary ingredient in passionately pursuing a life as a God worshiper. Jesus demonstrated that necessity, using scripture to fight off Satan's brazen attempts to gain the Son of God's worship.

"Again, the devil took Him to a very high mountain and showed Him all the kingdoms of the world and their glory; and he said to Him, 'All these things I will give You, if You fall down and worship me.' Then Jesus said to him, 'Go, Satan! For it is written, "YOU SHALL WORSHIP THE LORD YOUR GOD, AND SERVE HIM ONLY."' Then the devil left Him" (Matthew 4:8-11).

God obviously understands the struggles and temptations that come with our earthly strivings as His worshipers and rewards each victory along our journey with more of Himself. We need to keep responding to the God who longs to continue revealing Himself to us, by offering back to Him in humble worship all He has given to us. Then when the attacks come (and, oh, they will), we can be quick to respond like Shadrach, Meshach, and Abednego in our refusal to bow to another god, with the firm confidence that comes from intimately knowing, loving, and worshiping *the* God Most High. It's a moment-by-moment choice we all face to let God have His rightful place in the center of our lives and worship – to seek Him first and not second. Making an unyielding determination *now* to be a worshiper of the Almighty God allows us to then daily live out of that focus and passion, wholly dependent on the power and guidance of the Holy Spirit.

We see another picture of where our praise and worship to God must come from in Hebrews.

"Through Him then, let us continually offer up a sacrifice of praise to God, that is, the fruit of lips that give thanks to His name" (Hebrews 13:15).

This verse states that the *"sacrifice of praise to God"* comes from *"the fruit of lips that give thanks to His name."* Just as the fruit of a tree is a sign that the tree has healthy life flowing from its roots through its branches, the fruit of our lips is an indication of what flows from our heart, healthy or not. As Matthew said, *"For the mouth speaks out of that which fills the heart" (Matthew 12:34).* Worship is first and foremost a heart issue. It can only flow out of a heart that is filled and overflowing with love, devotion, and thanksgiving to God.

We can't look at this verse without reiterating why we, sinful humans, are even able to offer worship acceptable to a holy God. It's *"through Him . . . "* – through Jesus! Matt Redman writes, " . . . everything we could ever offer to God in worship has been provided by Him in the first place. But even forgetting the gifts themselves, the very means of our access into His presence is all of His own provision. It is a gifted response. We could never enter by our own efforts. We come to the Father on the merit of what Jesus has done. In light of the cross, the resurrection and the ascension, we come **through** Jesus, **in** Jesus and **with** Jesus. And we come too in the power of the Holy Spirit."[2] Apart from Jesus, we have absolutely nothing worthy to offer God in worship, and no access to His presence. And knowing that, He lovingly and graciously pours Himself out for us, so we can reap the blessings of pouring it all back out at His feet in return, in the form of worship.

The sacrifice that makes our *"sacrifice of praise"* possible was the one that *He* willingly made. Because of His shed blood on the cross on our behalf, we are no longer required to present a blood offering. Instead, our sacrifice comes in the form of bowed-down prayer, thanksgiving, and worship offerings in humble response to Him. What inconceivable, extravagant grace that allows us to even utter a single word in His presence! Apart from Christ, each word uttered is meaningless. Through Christ, it is a fragrant aroma, pleasing to the Father. *"For we are a fragrance of Christ to God among those who are being saved and among those who are perishing"* (*2 Corinthians 2:15*). The worship of a heart that stands right before God, offered through Jesus' work on its behalf, is always acceptable and pleasing in His sight.

David sang in Psalm 54:6, *"Willingly I will sacrifice to You; I will give thanks to Your name, O LORD, for it is good."* Any *"sacrifice"* of our time or focus that we may struggle with pales greatly once we get a glimpse of His greatness and goodness. And if we're weighing the cost of our sacrifice, then we're not sincerely entering worship. The *"willing"* sacrifice is a heartfelt expression of an intimate relationship with the God who has brought you out of your sinful pit and drawn you, awestruck and humbled, to your knees before Him. It's the result of passionately pursuing the Lord God Almighty who *first* passionately pursued you!

It's *who* we're pursuing that makes the pursuit matter. We only become authentic worshipers of God because of the absolute greatness of the God we worship and because of the pouring out of His grace and mercy on us. Only the greatness of the *focus* of our worship has the power to make our worship great. No secret formula, or even a diligent persistence at the spiritual disciplines, though good, can guarantee it. We need to stop often to be struck with wonder at His wonderfulness, with awe at His awesomeness, and with marvel at His marvelousness. Those aren't the passionate responses of people who are still unaware of their God. Only those who have truly encountered the Living God have their hearts and minds totally captured by amazement beyond earthly description. Warren Wiersbe says, "Wonder is not cheap amusement that brings a smile to your face. It is an encounter with reality, with God, which brings awe to your heart. You're overwhelmed with an emotion that is a mixture of gratitude, adoration, reverence, fear – and love. You're not looking for explanations; you're lost in the wonder of God."[3] We need to passionately pursue and encounter *that* God – the God of the Bible!

Take this time to gaze on Him now. Read the following verses of proclamation from His word aloud to Him – on your knees if possible.

" . . . *'Blessed are You, O LORD God of Israel our father, forever and ever. Yours, O LORD, is the greatness and the power and the glory and the victory and the majesty, indeed everything that is in the heavens and the earth; Yours is the dominion, O LORD, and You exalt Yourself as head over all. Both riches and honor come from You, and You rule over all, and in Your hand is power and might; and it lies in Your hand to make great and to strengthen everyone. Now therefore, our God, we thank You, and praise Your glorious name'"* (1 Chronicles 29:11-13).

"Your lovingkindness, O LORD, extends to the heavens, Your faithfulness reaches to the skies. Your righteousness is like the mountains of God; Your judgments are like a great deep. O LORD, You preserve man and beast. How precious is Your lovingkindness, O God! And the children of men take refuge in the shadow of Your wings. They drink their fill of the abundance of Your house; And You give them to drink of the river of Your delights. For with You is the fountain of life; In Your light we see light" (Psalm 36:5-9).

"I will cry to God Most High, To God who accomplishes all things for me" (Psalm 57:2).

"My soul, wait in silence for God only, For my hope is from Him. He only is my rock and my salvation, my stronghold; I shall not be shaken. On God my salvation and my glory rest; The rock of my strength, my refuge is in God. Trust in Him at all times, O people; Pour out your heart before Him; God is a refuge for us" (Psalm 62:5-8).

"Blessed be the Lord, who daily bears our burden, The God who is our salvation. God is to us a God of deliverances" (Psalm 68:19-20a).

"O LORD God of hosts, who is like You, O mighty LORD? Your faithfulness also surrounds You . . . The heavens are Yours, the earth also is Yours; The world and all it contains, You have founded them . . . You have a strong arm; Your hand is mighty, Your right hand is exalted. Righteousness and justice are the foundation of Your throne; Lovingkindness and truth go before You" (Psalm 89:8,11,13-14).

"O come, let us sing for joy to the LORD, Let us shout joyfully to the rock of our salvation. Let us come before His presence with thanksgiving, Let us shout joyfully to Him with psalms. For the LORD is a great God And a great King above all gods . . . Come, let us worship and bow down, Let us kneel before the LORD our Maker. For He is our God" (Psalm 95:1-3,6-7a).

"Praise the LORD! Praise, O servants of the LORD, Praise the name of the LORD. Blessed be the name of the LORD from this time forth and forever. From the rising of the sun to its setting the name of the LORD is to be praised. The LORD is high above all nations; His glory is above the heavens. Who is like the LORD our God, Who is enthroned on high, Who humbles Himself to behold the things that are in heaven and in the earth? . . . Praise the LORD!" (Psalm 113:1-6,9c).

"For a child will be born to us, a son will be given to us; And the government will rest on His shoulders; And His name will be called Wonderful Counselor, Mighty God, Eternal Father, Prince of Peace" (Isaiah 9:6).

"Behold, the Lord GOD will come with might, With His arm ruling for Him. Behold, His reward is with Him And His recompense before Him. Like a shepherd He will tend His flock, In His arm He will gather the lambs and carry them in His bosom; He will gently lead the nursing ewes. Who has measured the waters in the hollow of His hand, And marked off the heavens by the span, And calculated the dust of the earth by the measure, And weighed the mountains in a balance And the hills in a pair of scales? Who has directed the Spirit of the LORD, Or as His counselor has informed Him? With whom did He consult and who gave Him understanding? And who taught Him in the path of justice and taught Him knowledge and informed Him of the way of understanding? . . . Do you not know? Have you not heard? Has it not been declared to you from the beginning? Have you not understood from the foundations of the earth? It is He who sits above the circle of the earth, And its inhabitants are like grasshoppers, Who stretches out the heavens like a curtain And spreads them out like a tent to dwell in . . . 'To whom then will you liken Me That I would be his equal?' says the Holy One. Lift up your eyes on high And see who has created these stars, The One who leads forth their host by number, He calls them all by name; Because of the greatness of His might and the strength of His power, Not one of them is missing " (Isaiah 40:10-14, 21-22, 25-26).

"BEHOLD, THE VIRGIN SHALL BE WITH CHILD AND SHALL BEAR A SON, AND THEY SHALL CALL HIS NAME IMMANUEL," which translated means, "GOD WITH US" (Matthew 1:23).

"Then Jesus again spoke to them, saying, 'I am the Light of the world; he who follows Me will not walk in the darkness, but will have the Light of life'" (John 8:12).

"And the Word became flesh, and dwelt among us, and we saw His glory, glory as of the only begotten from the Father, full of grace and truth" (John 1:14).

"So Jesus said to them again, 'Truly, truly, I say to you . . . I am the door; if anyone enters through Me, he will be saved . . . I am the good shepherd; the good shepherd lays down His life for the sheep'" (John 10:7,9,11).

"Jesus said to him, 'I am the way, and the truth, and the life; no one comes to the Father but through Me'" (John 14:6).

"Oh, the depth of the riches both of the wisdom and knowledge of God! How unsearchable are His judgments and unfathomable His ways!" (Romans 11:33).

" . . . the mystery . . . is Christ in you, the hope of glory" (Colossians 1:26-27).

"I am the Alpha and the Omega, the first and the last, the beginning and the end" (Revelation 22:13).

"HOLY, HOLY, HOLY is THE LORD GOD, THE ALMIGHTY, WHO WAS AND WHO IS AND WHO IS TO COME. Worthy are You, our Lord and our God, to receive glory and honor and power; for You created all things, and because of Your will they existed, and were created" (Revelation 4:8b, 11).

"Then I looked, and I heard the voice of many angels around the throne and the living creatures and the elders; and the number of them was myriads of myriads, and thousands of thousands, saying with a loud voice, 'Worthy is the Lamb that was slain to receive power and riches and wisdom and might and honor and glory and blessing.' And every created thing which is in heaven and on the earth and under the earth and on the sea, and all things in them, I heard saying, 'To Him who sits on the throne, and to the Lamb, be blessing and honor and glory and dominion forever and ever'" (Revelation 5:11-13).

"And they sang the song of Moses, the bond-servant of God, and the song of the Lamb, saying, "Great and marvelous are Your works, O Lord God, the Almighty; Righteous and true are Your ways, King of the nations! 'Who will not fear, O Lord, and glorify Your name? For You alone are holy; For ALL THE NATIONS WILL COME AND WORSHIP BEFORE YOU, FOR YOUR RIGHTEOUS ACTS HAVE BEEN REVEALED'" (Revelation 15:3-4).

Now sit in stillness and silence – listening for His loving response back to you.

Don't rush.

Wait patiently.

Focus.

Listen.

Expect.

"Be still, and know that I am God" (Psalm 46:10).

That is the God of the Bible. *That* is the God who deserves all that we could possibly offer Him in worship. There are no other words, beyond what you just read from His Word, that I could possibly utter to further establish His worthiness of our worship.

The greatest journey of your life lies before you – the passionate pursuit of worshiping *the* Lord God Almighty! "God is trying to call us back to that for which He created us – to worship Him and to enjoy Him forever!" (A.W. Tozer).[4] Join me in answering His call. Engage in this incomparable journey with all your might. The humble privilege is beyond comprehension – the intimate reward exceeds description. It's the deepest hunger of your soul. And it's a taste of glorious eternity here on earth. Let the passionate pursuit begin!

Pause: to reflect and pray

What distractions do I have in my life that inhibit or prevent my worship, either in church or in my private spiritual walk? What worship-robbing tables need to be turned over in my life? (Consider life choices, sinful habits, attitudes, disinterest, etc.)

Find some Bible passages to memorize that you can use to combat those distractions when they occur, and write them here. (Don't hesitate to ask for help doing this if you need it.)

How does the story of Shadrach, Meshach, and Abednego challenge my view of worship?

Do I struggle to have a heart and mind set on seeking, knowing, loving, and worshiping God each day? If so, what steps am I willing to take to change that? Who can I ask to hold me accountable for this?

Do my lips consistently reflect a healthy heart that's focused on Him? Explain.

What was my response to reading the scripture passages about God aloud?

What steps will I take to grow in the knowledge and love of my awesome God and in my call to be His worshiper?

Pour out your heart to God in worship now, lifting up the truths about Him from the passages you just read, or anything else that He's laid on your heart to offer to Him in worship today. Encounter Him closely. Gaze on Him. Respond to Him. Pour everything out to Him that He's poured out for you. Bow before your God.

APPENDIX

Names, Titles, and Descriptions of God

According to the New International Version Bible
Holy Bible, New International Version®, NIV® Copyright © 1973, 1978, 1984, 2011
by Biblica, Inc.®

FATHER

A faithful God who does no wrong
A forgiving God
A fortress of salvation
A glorious crown
A jealous and avenging God
A Master in heaven
A refuge for his people
A refuge for the needy in his distress
A refuge for the oppressed
A refuge for the poor
A sanctuary
A shade from the heat
A shelter from the storm
A source of strength
A stronghold in times of trouble
An ever present help in trouble
Architect and builder
Builder of everything

Commander of the Lord's army
Creator of heaven and earth
Defender of widows
Eternal King
Father
Father of compassion
Father of our spirits
Father of the heavenly lights
Father to the fatherless
God **(El)**
God Almighty **(El-Shaddai)**
God and Father of our Lord Jesus Christ
God Most High **(El-Elyon)**
God my Maker
God my Rock
God my Savior
God my stronghold
God of Abraham, Isaac, and Jacob

God of all comfort
God of all mankind
God of glory
God of grace
God of hope
God of love and peace
God of peace
God of retribution
God of the living
God of the spirits of all
  mankind
God of truth
God our Father
God our strength
God over all the kingdoms of
  the earth
God the Father
God with us **(Immanuel)**
God who avenges me
God who gives endurance and
  encouragement
God who relents from sending
  calamity
God who sees **(El-Roi)**
Great and awesome God
Great and powerful God
Great, mighty and awesome
  God
He who blots out your
  transgressions
He who comforts you
He who forms the hearts of all
He who raised Christ from the
  dead
He who reveals his thoughts to
  man
Helper of the fatherless
Him who is able to do
  immeasurably more than all
  we ask or imagine

Him who is able to keep you
  from falling
Him who is ready to judge the
  living and the dead
Holy Father
Holy One
Holy One among you
I AM **(Hayah)**
I AM WHO I AM **(Hayah
  Asher Hayah)**
Jealous **(Qanna)**
Judge of all the earth
King of glory
King of heaven
Living and true God
Lord, Master **(Adonai)**
Lord Almighty
Lord God Almighty
Lord is Peace
  (Jehovah-Shalom)
Lord **(Yahweh, Jehovah)**
Lord Most High
Lord my Banner **(Jehovah Nissi)**
Lord my Rock
Lord of all the earth
Lord of heaven and earth
Lord of kings
Lord of Hosts/Powers
  (Jehovah Sabaoth)
Lord our God
Lord our Maker
Lord our Righteousness
  (Jehovah Tsidkenu)
Lord our Shepherd
  (Jehovah-Rohi)
Lord our shield
Lord who heals
  (Jehovah-Rapha)
Lord who is there **(Jehovah
  Shammah)**

Lord who makes you holy
  (Jehovah Mekoddishkem)
Lord who strikes the blow
Lord will Provide **(Jehovah
  Jireh)**
Love
Maker of all things
Maker of heaven and earth
Most High
My advocate
My Comforter in sorrow
My confidence
My help
My helper
My hiding place
My hope
My light
My mighty rock
My refuge in the day of disaster
My refuge in times of trouble
My song
My strong deliverer
My support
One to be feared
Only true God **(Elohim)**
Only wise God
Our dwelling place
Our judge
Our lawgiver
Our leader
Our Mighty One
Our Redeemer
Our refuge and strength
Righteous Father
Righteous judge
Rock of our salvation
Shepherd

Sovereign Lord
The Almighty
The compassionate and
  gracious God
The Eternal God
The consuming fire
The Everlasting God **(El Olam)**
The exalted God
The faithful God
The gardener (husbandman)
The glorious Father
The Glory of Israel
The God of the Covenant
  (El-Berith)
The God who saves me
The God who sees me
The great King above all gods
The just and mighty One
The living Father
The Majestic Glory
The Majesty in heaven
The one who sustains me
The only God
The potter
The rock in whom I take refuge
The spring of living water
The strength of my heart
The true God
You who hear prayer
You who judge righteously and
  test the heart and mind
You who keep your covenant of
  love with your servants
You who love the people
Your glory
Your praise
Your very great reward

JESUS

A banner for the peoples
A Nazarene
All
Alpha and Omega
Ancient of Days
Anointed One
Apostle and high priest
Author and perfecter of our faith
Author of life
Author of their salvation
Blessed and only Ruler
Branch of the Lord
Bread of God
Bread of life
Bridegroom
Chief cornerstone
Christ Jesus my Lord
Christ Jesus our hope
Christ of God
Consolation of Israel
Covenant for the people
Crown of splendor
Eternal life
Faithful and True
Faithful and true witness
First to rise from the dead
Firstborn from among the dead
Firstborn over all creation
First fruits of those that have fallen asleep
Fragrant offering and sacrifice of God
Friend of tax collectors and sinners
God of all the earth
God over all

God's Son
Great high priest
Great light
Great Shepherd of the sheep
Guarantee of a better covenant
He who comes down from heaven and gives life to the world
He who searches hearts and minds
Head of every man
Head of the body, the church
Head of the church
Head over every power and authority
Heir of all things
Him who died and came to life again
Him who loves us and has freed us from our sins
His one and only son
Holy and Righteous One
Holy One of God
Holy servant Jesus
Hope of Israel
Horn of salvation
Image of the invisible God
Immanuel (God with us)
Indescribable gift
Jesus
Jesus Christ
Jesus Christ our Lord
Jesus Christ our Savior
Jesus of Nazareth
Judge of the living and the dead
KING OF KINGS
King of the ages

Lamb of God
Light for revelation to the
  Gentiles
Light of life
Light of men
Light of the world
Living bread that came down
  from heaven
Lord and Savior Jesus Christ
Lord (Kurios)
Lord of glory
LORD OF LORDS
Lord of peace
Lord of the harvest
Lord of the Sabbath
Lord (Rabboni)
Man accredited by God
Man of sorrows
Master
Mediator of a new covenant
Merciful and faithful high
  priest
Messenger of the covenant
Messiah
Morning star
My friend
My intercessor
One who makes men holy
One who speaks to the Father
  in our defense
One who will arise to rule over
  the nations
Our glorious Lord Jesus Christ
Our God and Savior Jesus
  Christ
Our only Sovereign and Lord
Our Passover lamb
Our peace
Our righteousness, holiness,
  and redemption

Physician
Prince and Savior
Prince of Peace
Prince of princes
Prince of the hosts
Ransom for all men
Refiner and purifier
Resurrection and the life
Righteous Judge
Righteous man
Righteous One
Rock eternal (rock of ages)
Ruler of God's creation
Ruler of the kings of the earth
Savior of the world
Second man
Shepherd and Overseer of your
  souls
Son of Man
Son of the Blessed One
Son of the living God
Son of the Most High God
Source of eternal salvation
Sure foundation
Teacher
The Amen
The atoning sacrifice for our sins
The Beginning and the End
The bright Morning Star
The exact representation of his
  being
The first and the Last
The gate (door)
The good shepherd
The Head
The last Adam
The life
The Living One
The living Stone
The Lord Our Righteousness

The man from heaven
The man Jesus Christ
The most holy
The One and Only
The only God our Savior
The radiance of God's glory
The rising of the sun
  (Dayspring)
The stone the builders rejected
The testimony given in its
  proper time
The true light

The true vine
The truth
The way
The Word (logos)
True bread from heaven
Wisdom from God
Witness to the peoples
Wonderful Counselor
Word of God
Word of life
Your life
Your salvation

HOLY SPIRIT

A deposit (earnest)
Another Counselor
Breath of the Almighty
Holy One
Holy Spirit
Holy Spirit of God
Seal
Spirit of Christ
Spirit of counsel and of power
Spirit of faith
Spirit of fire
Spirit of glory
Spirit of God
Spirit of grace and supplication
Spirit of his Son
Spirit of holiness
Spirit of Jesus Christ

Spirit of judgment
Spirit of justice
Spirit of knowledge and of the
  fear of the Lord
Spirit of life
Spirit of our God
Spirit of the Lord
Spirit of the Sovereign Lord
Spirit of truth
Spirit of wisdom and of
  understanding
Spirit of wisdom and revelation
The gift
The promised Holy Spirit
The same gift
Voice of the Almighty
Voice of the Lord

ENDNOTES

Lesson 1

1. A.W. Tozer, *Whatever Happened to Worship?* (Christian Publications, 1985) p.9, 7
2. Warren W. Wiersbe, *Real Worship* (Baker Books, 2000), p.21
3. Paul Billheimer, *Destined for the Throne* (Christian Literature Crusade, 1975) p.121

Lesson 3

1. Warren Wiersbe, *Real Worship* (Baker Books, 2000), p.21
2. I got this illustration idea from the title of an article, though with a different focus, by Cathy Little called *"Diving with a Snorkel"*. http://www.worshipministry.com/worship-leader-devotional-going-deeper-diving-with-a-snorkel/
3. Matt Redman, *The Unquenchable Worshipper* (Regal Books, 2001), p.25
4. Ibid. p.71. Redman also quotes Anthony Bloom, *Beginning to Pray* (Mahwah, NJ: Paulist Press, 1982)
5. Ibid. p.72
6. Matt Redman, *"Let Everything That Has Breath"* (UK: Kingsway's Thankyou Music, n.d.).

Lesson 4

1. John Wimber quoting Carol Wimber, *Thoughts on Worship* (Vineyard Music Group, 1996), p.2
2. Laurie Klein, *"I Love You, Lord"*, (House of Mercy Music, 1978)

3. Gary Best, *Thoughts on Worship* (Vineyard Music Group, 1996), p.15

4. Matt Redman, *The Unquenchable Worshipper* (Regal Books, 2001), p.85

5. A.W.Tozer, *Whatever Happened to Worship?* (Christian Publications, 1985), p.44&46

6. If the Spirit-filled life is a new concept to you, check out www.cru.org/training-and-growth/classics/the-spirit-filled-life or http://www.cru.org/training-and-growth/classics/transferable-concepts/walk-in-the-spirit/index.htm.

Lesson 5

1. Warren W. Wiersbe, *Real Worship* (Baker Books, 2000), p.21

2. William Temple, *Readings in St. John's Gospel* (London Macmillan, 1939), p.68

3. John Wimber, *Thoughts on Worship* (Vineyard Music Group, 1996), p.3

4. Louie Giglio, *The Air I Breathe* (Multnomah Publishers, 2003), p.11

5. Matt Redman, *The Unquenchable Worshipper* (Regal Books, 2001), p.42

6. Ibid. p.53

Lesson 6

1. John Wimber, *Thoughts on Worship* (Vineyard Music Group, 1996), p.6

Lesson 7

1. Warren W. Wiersbe, *Real Worship* (Baker Books, 2000), p.15

2. Matt Redman, *The Unquenchable Worshipper* (Regal Books, 2001), p.62

3. Paul Billheimer, *Destined for the Throne* (Christian Literature Crusade, 1975) p.117

4. John Wimber, *Thoughts on Worship* (Vineyard Music Group, 1996), p.11

Lesson 8

1. Matt Redman, *The Unquenchable Worshipper* (Regal Books, 2001), p.27.
2. Warren W. Wiersbe, *Be Worshipful* (David C. Cook, 2004), p.207
3. A.W. Tozer, *Whatever Happened to Worship?* (Christian Publications, 1985), p.128

Lesson 9

1. Israel Houghton, speaking at Elevation Church in 2012. Podcast no longer found.
2. Matt Redman, *The Unquenchable Worshipper* (Regal Books, 2001), p.71
3. A.W. Tozer, *Whatever Happened to Worship?* (Christian Publications, 1985), p.14
4. Ibid. p.46

Lesson 10

1. Steven Furtick, founding pastor of Elevation Church, in a message called *"Guest of Honor"*, www.elevation-church.org/sermons/invitation
2. Matt Redman, *Facedown* (Regal Books, 2004), p.29-30
3. Warren W. Wiersbe, *Real Worship* (Baker Books, 2000), p.43
4. A.W. Tozer, *Whatever Happened to Worship?* (Christian Publications, 1985), p.12

Learn more about John and Pam Haddix's ministry
with Authentic Artist Resources at:

www.goauthentic.org

and

www.haddixes.org

PONDERINGS

Extra space for your reflections or prayers.

PONDERINGS

Extra space for your reflections or prayers.

PONDERINGS

Extra space for your reflections or prayers.

PONDERINGS

Extra space for your reflections or prayers.

PONDERINGS

Extra space for your reflections or prayers.